Preparing to Say

"I DO"

When Parents Said

"I DON'T"

Preparing to Say

"I DO"

When Parents Said

"I DON'T"

A PREMARITAL GUIDE FOR ADULTS WITH DIVORCED PARENTS

KENT DARCIE

For adults with divorced parents
who hope to have a successful marriage or remarriage,
but secretly fear it's not possible

CONTENTS

CONTENTS

PREFACE

Can We Have a Marriage That Lasts?

My parents' divorce has made me struggle with the idea of marriage, wondering, "If they can't make it work, will I be able to get married and make it work?"—almost like I'm afraid it's genetic.[1]

ACD #35, *Primal Loss*

Many adult children of divorce (ACDs) wonder if they'll be able to make their own marriages work. If that's you or someone you love, I'm excited to share some steps to help you (or them) avoid the mishaps that can often happen in marriage and lead to divorce.

The good news is, couples are 30 percent less likely to divorce if they participate in some premarital preparation.[2] The bad news is, too often, the impact of parental divorce is unaddressed in that process.

When my wife and I married forty-one years ago, my parents had been divorced for ten years. My father was in his second marriage, and Mom was unable to attend the wedding for reasons too numerous to detail here. We met with our pastor a couple of times, but nothing about my parents' divorce was addressed. This is unfortunate, because many of the issues common to ACDs that I'll address were negatively impacting me, and later our marriage.

As a licensed professional counselor (LPC), I sometimes see individuals or couples who are attending premarital counseling sessions through their churches. In most cases, basic marital and spiritual issues and tools are covered. However, rarely does a couple tell me that their mentor or leader asked about any impact their parents' divorce has had on them. The leader may ask questions about family structure, the early home environment, or even concerns about the parents' marriage, but often as a broad overview. The process typically doesn't involve exploring the layers of emotional impact parental divorce can create.

Questions like, Was the divorce triggered by an affair? are rarely broached. Yet a *yes* answer can signal the potential for decreased trust in a person's significant other, which puts extra stress on the relationship due to the ACD's suspicion and fear that it could happen to them.

Another fair question is, How is your trust in God? Research shows parental divorce can lower this in the affected children.[3] "Trust in the Lord with all your heart and do not lean on your own understanding" (Proverbs 3:5 ESV) becomes, "I can trust God, but . . ." After all, can we trust God if we believe He allowed our family to be destroyed? In order to achieve the goal of a God-honoring marriage, issues like this need to be discussed.

Genesis 2:24 says, "Therefore a man shall leave his father and his mother and hold fast to his wife, and they shall become one flesh" (ESV). Instead of "hold fast to his wife," other Bible versions say, "be united," "joined," or to "cleave." Each of these words suggest an unbreakable bond. I've even heard the analogy that compares this concept to gorilla glue.

However, the "glue" of adult children of divorce in marriage is often diluted by the fears, anger, and other issues from childhood that can weaken that sacred bond.

This book will help the process of identifying impurities in the "glue," enabling you to address them so your marriage bond will stick, "till death do us part."

Here are three important considerations for what you'll encounter in these pages:

First, this book will not disparage divorced parents. Ephesians 6:2 (quoting Deuteronomy 5:15) says, "'Honor your father and mother'—which is the first commandment with a promise" (NIV). My position is threefold. 1) The divorce happened. 2) It's important to explore the impact of the divorce on the kids when they're grown. 3) Once the impact is identified, we need to learn how to overcome that impact and create healthy relationships and marriages.

Second, I'm not throwing stones at anyone who works to help couples lay a strong foundation for a lasting marriage. Many are unaware of the negative impact parental divorce can have on the stability and longevity of a marriage.

If you've never paused to consider the impact of your parents' divorce on you, I get it. I've found, and numerous sources support, that denial is rampant among adults with divorced parents, so the issues that can affect them are often masked—especially during the dating or engagement period. *I'm good. The holidays are a hassle, but I'm just fine*, is the mantra.

Part of this is due to society's belief that parental divorce is a mere bump in the road with minimal lasting consequences. But the embarrassment, shame, and concerns over "not airing dirty laundry" also foster a move-on mindset.

Lauren Reitsema, an adult child of divorce, touches on yet another reason in her book *In Their Shoes: Helping Parents Better Understand and Connect with Children of Divorce*. She explains:

> Children are given a lot of credit in their role after a divorce. They are quickly labeled as resilient and malleable, adaptable and strong. This creates pressure to move on without the necessary social supports required to fully address the pain. Often in the faith community, rushing

the grief timelines seems to be supported with spiritual taglines: *God has a plan. God wouldn't give you more than you can handle.*[3]

My twenty-plus years of identifying and addressing issues faced by adult children of divorce has shown that the majority of the time these issues aren't known, so it's unlikely a discussion of the impact of the parents' divorce will come up naturally.

The third note about this book involves its focus.

TYPES OF DIVORCES

Spectrum of Parental Divorce

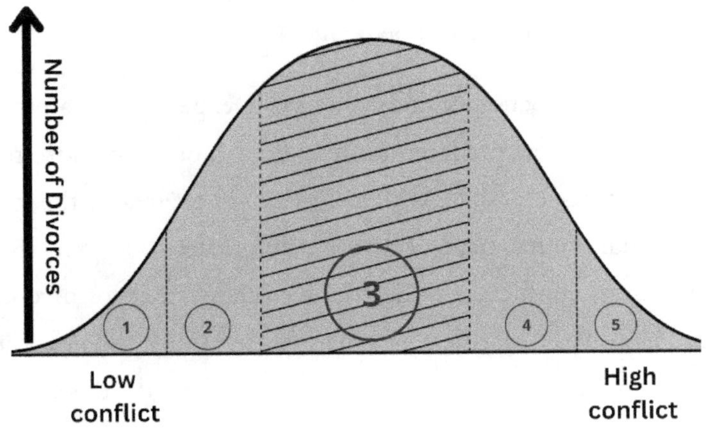

The chart above identifies the various types of parental divorce that ACDs experience.

Areas 1 and 2 represent divorces in low-conflict marriages. In these divorces, the couples remain so friendly that you might wonder why they divorced at all. Areas 4 and 5 represent divorces in high-conflict marriages. For example, marriages in which a partner had an affair are represented in area 4, while area 5 represents marriages where issues like neglect, abuse, addictions, serious mental health disorders, and the like, are present.

Roughly 70 percent of divorces are represented in the center section, area 3. Reasons for these divorces include:

- "We had irreconcilable differences."
- "We grew apart."
- "We were never in love."
- "I need to be happy."
- "My needs weren't being met."

This book focuses on individuals who experienced parental divorces that were predominantly in area 3, but also addresses those in areas 2 and 4. The closer you get to area 1, the less conflictual the marriage or divorce. The closer you get to area 5, the more conflictual or destructive the marriage or divorce was. However, regardless of where your family falls on the graph, you're likely experiencing an impact from the divorce—usually negative.

E. Mavis Hetherington, author of *For Better or for Worse: Divorce Reconsidered,* wrote that "Marrying a person from an intact family significantly reduces the higher risk of marital instability carried by ACDs."[4]

Pretty scary quote, huh? But *please hear me!* If you have divorced parents, you are not broken or doomed to a failed marriage. If you're from an intact family, you don't have to freak out. That quote reflects the sad truth that millions of ACDs like me didn't have a resource like this.

Hetherington's quote also addresses a possible reason why some of you are remarrying. You were unaware of the issues that resulted from your parents' divorce, and here you are. But, regardless of what led you here, you are pages away from launching your next marriage in a healthier way.

Whether you're marrying or remarrying, I believe combining the traditional focus of premarital counseling with identifying the impact parental divorce has had on an individual greatly enhances a person's ability to start their marriage on the strongest possible foundation.

However, you may find that this book raises difficult issues. In some cases, it may be helpful to seek the assistance of a professional counselor.

Finally, there are questions at the end of each chapter. Don't skip past them! They will open doors to areas that may need healing.

This book is not intended to go into the topics that follow in great depth or serve as a replacement for traditional marriage-preparation tools. Here, I will identify common issues that impact adults with divorced parents. The resource section in the back of the book includes materials that can help you do a deeper dive.

QUESTIONS

1. Which of the five areas best represents your parents' divorce on the Types of Divorce chart? Give specific reasons why you made your choice.
2. In what ways do you believe your parents' divorce has impacted (or is impacting) you?

First Things First: Identifying the Issues

The wedding planner suspected something when the bride-to-be asked if her mother had to be seated in the front row. "No, she doesn't. It is customary, but more and more weddings are handling the event in less traditional ways." Having experienced these types of questions before, she continued, "Is there a particular reason you're asking?"

"Just curious," the bride responded. But both ladies knew there was much more than curiosity involved.

Later that evening, after their consult with the wedding planner, the bride- and groom-to-be, Jamie and Garrison, attended a premarital counseling session with their pastor and his wife. The engaged couple sat in comfortable chairs, alternating between glee and embarrassment as they worked through that week's topic: handling finances.

Reading from a counseling text, the pastor asked, "Would you rather spend money on food, clothes, décor, or activities?"[1] As the husband-wife team taught about the different ways people approach finances, Jamie's mind drifted: *Garrison is a great guy, but could he wander off like my dad did? The podcast I listened to said all men are weak. Should I separate my money, so I don't get caught off guard like my mother if the marriage fails? What if Garrison gets tired of the circus my family is? What could someone so perfect see in me? Garrison has no idea what a mess I am.*

Her mental list went on, but none of those issues would be touched in their six weeks of marriage-preparation classes. Yet, the bride's anxiety was increasing with each session.

WHEN SIMPLE IS COMPLEX

Jamie and Garrison represent a composite of many couples and situations. Names from around the globe could have been used. But one thing is common to the majority of them: "Simple" issues are often complicated with divorced parents. For example, here was part of Jamie's guest list:

- her mom,
- mom's new boyfriend,
- dad,

- dad's wife,
- brother and his wife,
- sister,
- and her grandmother.

Sounds simple enough, right? The actual list looks like this, though:

- her mom,
- mom's new boyfriend—whom Dad always makes sarcastic comments about,
- dad,
- his wife—the woman he had the affair with,
- Bryan, the brother who faithfully stood by their dad through the whole mess,
- Bryan's wife—whose divorced parents nearly caused them to elope,
- sister, Sarah, who will talk to Dad, but not his wife even after four years of their marriage,
- and her grandma, who hasn't spoken to her dad since the affair was revealed.

Now do you see why she's thinking, *What if Garrison gets tired of my family's circus?* Are you starting to get a feel for some of the complex dynamics that are in play and will still be in play days, months, and years after the wedding?

Will this lead Jamie to try to be the perfect wife? We don't know. What we *do* know is that it's likely she doesn't realize how she's being impacted by basic issues that can affect adults with divorced parents, issues that can thwart her efforts to be the "perfect wife." These may include struggles in the following areas:

- Anger
- Trusting people
- Unforgiveness
- Reconciling biblical truth with their family circumstances
- Fears, including fear of conflict, abandonment, feeling inadequate/inferior, divorce, or doom (the belief that bad things will happen at any moment)

A fear of doom can plague ACDs even when there's no evidence to support it. Sometimes it's described as *waiting for the other shoe to drop.* Ironically, this fear of loss can increase as things get better. This sounds counterintuitive, but when a person subconsciously believes that things can fall apart at any moment, there is more to lose if things are going well.

The major problem? This list contains the very issues that weaken a marriage. What if both of you are experiencing them? It's not uncommon for one ACD to be drawn to another ACD because they understand and can empathize with each other.

SOME STATISTICS TO CONSIDER

This may, in part, help to explain research discussed in Nicolas H. Wolfinger's book *Understanding the Divorce Cycle*. As a researcher and expert on parent-child relationships, he found,

> Children-of-divorced-parents are at least 50 percent more likely to get a divorce than those from an unbroken home. When both the husband and wife come from divorced families, the odds of divorce are 200 percent higher than those from an intact home.[2]

This doesn't include kids that experience parental breakups in cohabitation or, as is often the case, multiple cohabitations, which results in serial simulated divorces.

Additionally, research on intergenerational transmission of relationship instability showed that "on average, children from single-parent families have a 190% higher risk to dissolve their first union during five years from its beginning."[3] Simply put, growing up in a divorced family increases the risk of divorce.[4]

I share this information not to depress you, but to challenge you to incorporate the reality of these statistics into your marriage preparation. This will enable you and your partner to work together strategically with the goal of creating a marriage that lasts.

Other factors can also negatively impact marriage. Terry Gaspard and Tracy Clifford, authors of *Daughters of Divorce,* cite a study showing that

> daughters of divorce expressed higher levels of mistrust with partners, less relationship satisfaction, [and] were more ambivalent about getting involved in a committed relationship compared to counterparts raised in intact homes or sons of divorce.[5]

They also cite a study conducted by Sarah Whitton of Boston University, indicating that

> daughters of divorce were more ambivalent about remaining committed to their partners and had less confidence in their ability to keep their marriage together compared to counterparts from intact homes—even after they accepted a proposal to wed.[6]

Citing E. Mavis Hetherington, Gaspard and Clifford continue:

> Hetherington's study demonstrates that the root of marital instability is that adult children of divorce are more likely to see divorce as an option to marital problems or even sporadic periods of unhappiness than other people are.[7]

Few ACDs are aware that these matters are running around their brains like a computer virus. Consequently, they are vulnerable to divorce and not realizing why.

A lack of modeling—the opportunity to observe what a healthy marriage looks like—is also problematic. It's common for adult children of divorce to witness little or no positive modeling due, in part, to the divorce itself, but also because of the difficulties remarriages and the resulting blended families can experience—both within the new family unit and as a result of contact with the previous spouses.

DOES FAITH HELP?

Perhaps you've wondered if people of faith fare better than their secular peers. Yes, but Christian couples that include ACDs may find it challenging to remain in church. A 2013 report by the Institute for American values noted, "A study by Leora E. Lawton and Regina Bures found that Catholic and moderate Protestant children of divorce are more than twice as likely to leave religious practice altogether, and that conservative Protestants are more than three times as likely to do so."[8]

Second, if the ACD does go to church regularly, their faith in what the Bible teaches may not be as solid as they profess. Elizabeth Marquardt addresses this quandary in her book *Between Two Worlds*. She writes,

I asked these young people from divorced families to reflect on the commandment to honor your father and mother. The children of divorce would get stuck. First of all, the commandment implies their parents were a unit, which theirs were not. It was very easy for them to honor a parent who stuck with them through thick and thin and sacrificed a lot for them—maybe a single mom or sometimes a single dad. Honoring that parent was no problem, but how do you honor the parent who left you? What does that mean? What does that mean as you get older and you're not so needy and vulnerable anymore? Or when the parents become the vulnerable ones? How do you make sense of all that?[9]

What tends to happen is these ACDs believe that God is the one who failed, not the one or two parents who made poor choices.

However, researcher and author Glenn Stanton cites research from Harvard's School of Public Health that shows "regularly attending church services together reduces a couple's risk of divorce by a remarkable 47 percent. Many studies, they report, have similar results ranging from 30 to 50 percent reduction in divorce risk."[10] Stanton further mentions that

Professor Annette Mahoney of Bowling Green's Spirituality and Psychology Research Team reports from her decades-long research that a couple's spiritual intimacy and church participation is "very, very important and undeniably a construct that matters" greatly in boosting marital happiness and longevity.[11]

Dealing with ACD issues is important for any couple in which one partner, or both, have experienced parental divorce. Addressing these issues in a biblical way is even more so. Why? Because God can soften the hardest heart, overcome the greatest challenge, and heal emotional wounds that seem unhealable. The problem is, when our emotional pain level exceeds the level of our faith in God's abilities, we can miss this truth. We start to believe that God can't supply our needs, though the Bible says, "My God will supply all your needs according to His riches in glory in Christ Jesus" (Philippians 4:19 NASB). Then we file for divorce.

In many cases, that's what I've seen. People follow in their parents' footsteps, though they once swore, "I'll never do that to my kids." Emotional pain from a difficult relationship causes us to move from "we can overcome this" to "*now* I understand why Dad left Mom," or vice versa.

But we don't have to replicate what we experienced. We have a choice. My father was an adult child of divorce, as was his father and grandfather. My dad had divorced twice and was heading toward his third marriage when God jolted me with the message (at a marriage conference) that I was on the same emotional path as my dad.

This was twenty years after my parents' divorce. I was thirty-three, had three kids, and struggled with many of the issues I've described. So my marriage was struggling—thus the marriage conference.

But God . . . aren't those wonderful words? God led me to resources that helped me identify and overcome the dominance of parental-divorce issues in my life—though some are pretty persistent! Adult Children of Divorced Parents Ministries was birthed out of my journey and 2 Corinthians 1:3–4.

> All praise to God, the Father of our Lord Jesus Christ. God is our merciful Father and the source of all comfort. He comforts us in all our troubles so that we can comfort others. When they are troubled, we will be able to give them the same comfort God has given us.

Take heart that there is no issue God can't help you with, regardless of the cause of your parents' divorce or how it unfolded. Remember this because in chapters 3, 4, and 5 we'll look at two of the thornier challenges ACDs can face. But first, we need to delineate the difference between the impact of parental divorce that occurs during our childhood versus that which occurs after we're adults.

QUESTIONS

1. Which of the issues we've discussed in this chapter may be areas of challenge for you? Explain why.

2. Which issues does your partner think are areas of challenge for you? Have them explain why, and listen with an open heart. James 1:19 applies here: "Everyone should be quick to listen, slow to speak and slow to become angry" (NIV).

CHAPTER 2

Experiencing Parental Divorce as an Adult (Gray Divorce)

*Nothing tested me more in my adult life than my parents'
split. . . . I was 26 years old at the time. I had moved out of my
childhood home to attend college several years before. I was in
a long-term relationship. I had a great job and a small circle
of close friends. My parents weren't sick or dying. I had all
of the things that should make you feel rooted. Yet, when my
parents announced they were separating, I felt as if the world
had collapsed in on me.*[1]

—Brook Lea Foster, *The Way They Were*

One thirty-year-old whose parents divorced when she
was an adult shared, "I get flashbacks to idyllic family

holidays and think, was that all just a front? Were we ever really the happy family I thought we were?"[2]

Gray divorce is the term for when parents divorce after the kids have grown. The children in these circumstances are affected in different ways than those who experienced their parents' divorce in childhood. And this group is growing rapidly. Depending on the source, up to 33 percent of divorces today involve those over fifty—the empty-nest crowd.[2]

Many carry the misconception that grown children experience little or no impact when their parents divorce. However, University of Toronto Professor Michael Saini identified five negative effects that often occur when adult children face gray divorce, and each is worth pausing to consider:

1. Feeling that they experienced a fake childhood
2. The difficulty of loyalty challenges as both parents turn to them for comfort and support
3. Anxiety about the success of their own relationships
4. Feeling isolated and that they lack sufficient support
5. Role boundary problems with their parents[3]

Let's take a closer look at each of those dynamics and how they can affect those who experienced their parents' divorce in their adulthood.

Feeling that they experienced a fake childhood. This can cause people to reexamine every piece of their childhood puzzle.

I've heard it described as taking a jigsaw puzzle, throwing it up in the air, and when it lands trying to rebuild it, wondering if the pieces fit where you thought they did before.

The difficulty of loyalty challenges. These occur because parents may expect their grown children to understand why the other parent is impossible to live with. Each believes it's a no-brainer, and the adult child should be on their side. This can create very difficult dynamics if the adult child stays neutral or, worse, chooses "the enemy's" side.

Anxiety about the success of one's own relationships. This can be difficult to avoid. The Bible says, "In all circumstances take up the shield of faith, with which you can extinguish all the flaming darts of the evil one" (Ephesians 6:16 ESV). Some of the Enemy's most effective darts are filled with doubt. A natural posture when one's parents stayed married is, *If Mom and Dad can make it with their issues, we can find a way to survive ours.* However, when parents divorce after thirty-five, forty, forty-five, or even fifty years, that view can change. *If they couldn't make it after all these years, how can we make it with all of our problems?* Anxiety and doubt creep in. And with them, when the troubles come—and they will in every marriage—the mindset can change from "Therefore what God has joined together, let not man separate," (Mark 10:9 NKJV) to, *Now I see why Mom left Dad.*

Feelings of isolation. These are very common among adult kids experiencing gray divorce, because friends and relatives don't understand the monumental shift that's occurred in their life and family. And the emotional and cognitive cost is often overlooked.

Isolation can result from emotional conflict. Author Brooke Lea Foster shares, "For me, knowing Mom and Dad were divorcing was devastating enough, but dealing with Mom, who expected me to be happy for her for leaving Dad, was even more emotionally draining."[4]

We may isolate ourselves when too many divergent stressors occur simultaneously. Hughes and Fredenburg reflect this in their guide for adult children experiencing gray divorce:

> Our kids are asking us what is happening with grandma and grandpa. I am distracted and having a lot of difficulty focusing at work. Both Mom and Dad call me at work, complaining about the other. Mom even calls and keeps inviting me to have dinner with her and her "boyfriend." That's what she calls him! Her "boyfriend"! Is there a word other than that? It's crazy![5]

These and myriad other issues make us feel like we're on a sinking island and all alone. It can help to remember verses like Psalm 61:2: "From the end of the earth I will cry to You, when my heart is overwhelmed; Lead me to the rock that is higher than I" (NKJV).

So, feeling that our childhood was fake, experiencing loyalty challenges, stressing over our own relationships, and feeling isolated can put undue stress on the marriage relationship unless addressed intentionally. But the last issue Professor Saini mentions can create even more stress.

Role boundary problems. Boundary challenges can pop up like weeds with gray divorce. Who is responsible for Dad now that he's eating burritos and soda every day for breakfast, lunch, and dinner? Do you want your kids to meet Grandma's new boyfriend? Are you going to have two birthday parties for your daughter because your parents can't be in the same room anymore? Who decides whether you and your family go to the annual summer trip (that you've attended since you were four) with "her" family? Can you shut down TMI (too much personal information) from a parent without feeling guilty?

Boundaries are essential, but not easy. To use boundaries successfully, it is important to know what boundaries are and how they work. In this context, boundaries are used to modify or eliminate troubling behaviors. However, before we can use a boundary, four steps must occur. A boundary is first created, then communicated, then implemented and, lastly, enforced. Because boundaries are usually created without the first three steps, the lack of enforcement is often where the boundary fails.

It's also important to remember that healthy boundaries (as opposed to capricious ones) are loving *and* biblical. God is love, and we see His use of boundaries in the second chapter of the Bible: "But the LORD God warned him, 'You may freely eat the fruit of every tree in the garden—except the tree of the knowledge of good and evil. If you eat its fruit, you are sure to die'" (Genesis 2:16–17). God set this boundary, and there were consequences when Adam and Eve disregarded it.

Boundaries are necessary in many parental-divorce situations, but with the lack of awareness many parents have regarding the impact of their gray divorce, it is essential to be equipped with strong boundary skills. One of the strongest resources on this topic is a book called *Boundaries* by Dr. Henry Cloud and Dr. John Townsend. This book is a must for those with divorced parents.[6]

While these five areas Professor Saini lists affect many adults whose parents divorce after they are grown, this is just a brief summary. We love our parents, but circumstances can strain that love. Again, the Bible says, "Therefore a man shall leave his father and his mother and hold fast to his wife, and they shall become one flesh" (Genesis 2:24 ESV). Leaving and cleaving while honoring our father and mother (Ephesians 6:2) can be a delicate dance for those touched by gray divorce. But acknowledging the issues and working through them as a couple can help mitigate the impact of any negative experiences we encounter.

QUESTIONS

1. Which of the five areas that affect those impacted by gray divorce do you identify with most? Explain how and why this area (or areas) challenge(s) you.
2. Which one do you think should be addressed first?

CHAPTER 3

The Struggle with Anger

Refrain from anger and turn from wrath;
do not fret—it leads only to evil.

Proverbs 37:8 NIV

And be sure of this: I am with you always,
even to the end of the age.

Matthew 28:20

A few years ago, my family was staying at a campground. While I was standing along one of the roads that ran alongside the campsites, a couple walked by. The teenage boy was walking at a brisk pace, and he was angry and yelling about something. Following about eight steps behind him was a teenage girl I assumed was his girlfriend. Every few steps, he would look back at her and call her every name in the book. This young girl just continued to follow him, head down, not saying anything.

Granted, I didn't know the situation, but as the father of a daughter, I watched them, thinking, *Why is she following this guy?*

In hindsight with the research I've done, while I can't say this as a fact, I would guess that those two precious young people were children from broken homes. The boy, filled with anger, was being followed by a girl filled with father hunger.

I'm devoting special attention to these two issues because, while they can affect both men and women who experienced parental divorce, anger tends to result in more destructive behaviors in men, and father hunger tends to produce more destructive behaviors in women. However, both can have a negative impact on the marriage if not addressed. This chapter will address anger. The following two chapters will look at father hunger in men and women, respectively.

THE ANGER CHALLENGE

Why can't I have a normal wedding like everyone else? Have you asked this question yet? *Actually, yes, Kent, but I'm not angry about it.*

In his book *Anger Is a Choice*, Tim LaHaye lists words we use instead of *anger*. A sampling includes *hot, irked, disgusted, cranky, fed up, annoyed, irritated, worked up, hurt,* and *mad.*[1]

If you are angry (or one of those other words), you're not alone. Research by Solangel Maldonado, a leader in addressing divorce issues in children, writes, "Children of divorce often deal with their anger in destructive ways, and those exposed to interparental anger are even less likely to know how to cope with anger in a healthy manner." Maldonado further notes, "Children's anger is not only intense, but for some, it *endures for decades* after their parents' divorce"[2] (emphasis mine).

This is where the anger-related impact of parental divorce can skew toward males. Maldonado goes on to say, "Children, like adults, unconsciously use anger to shield themselves from the emotional hurt they are experiencing. It may be easier to express anger than to admit feeling sad, afraid, or rejected."[3] While men and women can experience anger, women are more likely to express other emotions.

So where does this anger come from?

SOURCES OF ANGER

Adult children of divorce may struggle to identify the sources of their anger. Here are some likely culprits to consider, some that may have sprung up in childhood if parental divorce occurred then.

Loss. Many losses accompany parental divorce—such as the loss of parental availability, the same standard of living, access to friends, or our ability to participate in extracurricular activities. Often, we're not happy about these losses, and anger can result.

Blame. Even if our parents' divorce didn't involve infidelity, addiction, or abuse, we still tend to pick sides. Blame and resentment can feed anger toward whomever we think is the guilty party.

The Loyalty Test. We can receive nonverbal and verbal cues from parents that cause us to feel we have to choose which parent we love more. The loyalty test is common and frustrating because we feel like we're in a no-win situation—because we are—and that often stirs anger.

Lack of control after the divorce. Prior to divorce, parents are child-centric. Schedules, resources, and so forth tend to revolve around the kids. After divorce, parents are parent-centric, where routines tend to revolve around the parents. Children can struggle with this change and respond in angry ways.

Fear. Fear can be a strong trigger for anger. For example, if you have a fear of abandonment and your spouse is delayed coming home, your fear can ignite into anger at them. As they walk in the door, they're blasted with, *"Where have you been?!"* What if we add a parent's affair to the mix. Now imagine what you might think when your spouse is late. In many cases, we don't connect our anger to fear. We just know we're angry.

Absorbed Anger. Maldonado notes, "Children sense their parents' emotions and often model their parents' behavior. As many as one-third of all divorces are accompanied by high levels of interparental hostility, and in as many as 25% of families, this conflict continues for years after the divorce is final."[4]

Proverbs 22:24–25 warns us about associating with people with quick tempers, stating, "Keep away from angry, short-tempered people, lest you learn to be like them and endanger your soul" (TLB). But, as Maldonado states, the angry and short-tempered were probably one or both of our parents.[5]

In her book *The Good Divorce*, Constance Ahrons observed that 50 percent of her research sample included divorced/divorcing couples she considered Angry Associates and Fiery Foes.[6] These are the ones that struggle to apply co-parenting skills.

So, a lot of anger may be present in children in the aftermath of divorce (implosive or bottled up and explosive). Learning is more often caught than taught, and kids can pick up anger from both the family atmosphere and through observation.

Stepparents. As children of divorce, we can get upset when we think a new stepparent is trying to replace the one we consider our primary parent. Anger can also arise because the focus of our parent's primary attention transfers from us to them. Last but not least, if a stepparent grabs the role of applying discipline too quickly, powerful anger may be triggered.

This is just a broad overview of anger-related issues. There are others, but it's important to identify any anger you carry, because its destructive nature will likely arise in marriage if not addressed.

Maldonado found, "Children's anger is not only intense, but for some, it endures for decades after their parents' divorce."[7] I've heard this from people I've spoken with and I have experienced it personally. Unresolved anger is often listed as a primary issue in the ACD's experience, and they may drag it into adulthood.

When I speak to clients about the impact of anger on our relationships, I refer to the Corningware plates and bowls from my childhood home. This dinnerware was virtually indestructible. If a plate dropped on the floor, it very rarely broke. However, if one did, it seemed to disintegrate into a zillion small, sharp pieces. Angry words can break a loved one's heart the same way.

The apostle Paul's letter to the early church in Colossae warns us about the power and impact anger can have in our relationships. "But now you must put them all away: anger, wrath, malice, slander, and obscene talk from your mouth" (Colossians 3:8 ESV). This is a very important issue to address before the ring goes on!

LAUNCH POINTS FOR ADDRESSING ANGER

Admit that you have anger. We've only looked at a handful of the countless anger triggers parental divorce can produce. If you have divorced parents, there's a high probability you carry related anger.

Acknowledge that anger is a choice. Some say, "Hot tempers just run in my family." This doesn't matter, because anger is a choice. Do you yell at your boss at work? Not likely. Most of us would *choose* not to because of the possible consequences.

Seek resources to help. Good books like Gary Chapman's *Anger: Handling a Powerful Emotion in a Healthy Way*[8] can help with working through triggers and processing them in ways that benefit us and our future spouse.

Reviewing Bible verses that address anger is a strong tool for guiding us as well. Examples include:

People with understanding control their anger; a hot temper shows great foolishness. (Proverbs 14:29)

My dear brothers and sisters, take note of this: Everyone should be quick to listen, slow to speak and slow to become angry, because human anger does not produce the righteousness that God desires. (James 1:19-20 NIV)

Love is patient and kind; love does not envy or boast; it is not arrogant or rude. It does not insist on its own way; it is not irritable or resentful. (1 Corinthians 13:4-5 ESV)

Scriptures like these can help you to learn the difference between righteous (godly) anger and unrighteous (self-focused) anger in the Bible.

Professional counseling, which can provide an objective view and effective anger management tools, can also be invaluable in this area.

Remind yourself that God is in control. The months leading up to the wedding can be stressful even without divorced parents. With them, frustrations can seem insurmountable. But the Bible assures us that God is with us and will continue to be after the wedding when life's challenges continue.

I mentioned that fear contributes to anger. One of my favorite scriptures helps with anxiety, which is usually fear-based. Philippians 4:6–7 says,

> Do not be anxious about anything, but in every situation, by prayer and petition, with thanksgiving, present your requests to God. And the peace of God, which transcends all understanding, will guard your hearts and your minds in Christ Jesus. (NIV)

I like these verses because they don't just tell us to not be anxious. They tell us *how* to not be. Take your concern to God. Apply these verses to all you're facing and cling to the promise they offer!

QUESTIONS

1. Has anyone ever suggested that you may have anger issues? What were the circumstances that led them to draw this conclusion?
2. How much anger did you see in your home before, during, and after your parents' divorce?
3. In your life, has your anger resulted in any negative consequences (e.g., job loss; relationship loss, stresses, or strain; hypertension; addictions; etc.)?

CHAPTER 4

How Father Hunger Can Impact Men

Even though I have been blessed to have such dynamic women in my life, only a man can impart some things to a son.[1]
—Steven Banks, *Healing the Father-Wound*

The choir was ready and the piano started to play. In high school, choir wasn't as cool as playing sports, but the young man enjoyed singing and was good at it. Glancing toward the doors one last time, he looked for a surprise visit from his father. His mother and sisters were always there, but oh, how he wished his father could see him showcase his skills! He never shared this secret wish with anyone. It was just as well, since his hopes were dashed again. To be fair, his father lived several hours away, but the disappointment was real. I know. That young man was me.

This chapter and the one that follows are important for both men and women to read. Ladies, these insights about what may be happening inside your future groom will enable you to support, respect, and build him up each day.

Men, you are called to protect, support, and cherish your bride. This is best done by understanding where her vulnerabilities and needs lie, so you can be a daily conduit for God's healing. So, again, I encourage each of you to read both father hunger chapters.

Margo Maine writes, "*Father hunger* is a deep, persistent desire for emotional connection with the father that is experienced by all children."[2] That emotional connection is difficult when the father's presence with the kids drops, or stops altogether.

Author Edward Teyber points out that researchers found only around 25 percent of children had weekly contact with their divorced fathers, about 20 percent saw these fathers only once or twice a year, and 55 percent had not seen them even once in the preceding twelve months.[3] The increase of 50/50 joint custody is helping to improve these numbers, but in most cases the father is around, at best, roughly half of the time.

For men, the lack of a father's presence can fuel a skewed view of what it is to be a man and father. As with many things, learning how to be a man is more caught than taught. If dad is gone at least 50 percent of the time, there is 50 percent less time for a son to catch important lessons from him. This is critical, because what a son does see and hear can be distorted in a number of ways.

As sons, we may have fathers tightroping between ex-wives, girlfriends, and subsequent wives, which can portray an image of instability or false bravado.

Nearly 70 percent of divorces are filed by women, which may raise another challenge. Sons might hear Mom, who isn't thrilled with the father at that point, talking with friends about "how men are," or worse, doing a verbal vomit on how bad a son's father is and why. After the divorce, "You're just like your father," has an extremely negative bite to it.

Additionally, mothers filter life through a female grid. This is not because of malice or some evil plot, but because Mom *is* female and sees things from a woman's reference point. Jesus said, "But from the beginning of creation, 'God made them male and female'" (Mark 10:6 ESV). Mothers tend to be risk averse and fathers risk-takers. Together, a healthy medium usually develops. But after the divorce, characteristics typically exhibited by males can be frowned upon if mothers aren't careful. And this can distort the image of a man for sons.

A distorted view of men and fathers can also be encouraged by changes for the worse in our father's behavior. Marriage tends to keep spouses in balance. With divorce, you now have two individuals who can do what they want unchecked. So, we may see multiple relationships, unreliable support, missed visitations or special events, and other unhealthy characteristics/behavior of what it means to be a man, husband, and father.

If the father is a man of faith, the distortion can be more problematic. Though Dad was once active and devoted to his church, now he may rarely go or speak of spiritual things. Or worse, some of his behaviors may be unbiblical. This can be confusing and disheartening to us as sons.

Most boys and young men want to admire their dads. Even fathers with significant struggles are super in our eyes. Mentally, we'll make excuses for shortcomings—even big ones like alcoholism, drug addiction, or philandering. The Bible says, "Love covers a multitude of sins" (1 Peter 4:8), and most boys are filled with love and admiration for their dads.

But this love can be buried under the negatives in circumstances or under the weight of the emotional pain we feel from various losses. Consequently, the power of a dad's influence is overshadowed by the model of a man touted by the media and friends, or we try to be men by faking it till we make it.

Ultimately, boys and the men they become are looking for the answer to one fundamental question: *Am I a real man?* We want to know that we are adequate.

One ACD affirmed this when he shared annoyance at feeling the need to prove his masculinity. Though happily married with a family and a successful career, he struggled with this nagging doubt: *Do I have what it takes to be a real man?* He was raised by his mother, who he assures did a great job, but the uncertainty remains.

If you want a feel for this dilemma, try googling "What is a real man like?" The answer depends on whether you look at a list created by women or men, liberals or conservatives, the educated or self-taught, religious or nonreligious, wounded or secure, those with Eastern or Western ideology, and so on. Is a real man a "ladies' man" or a someone who protects a woman's heart? For sons, the answer usually starts with our fathers.

Doubts about manhood can surface when a man enters the realm of serious dating. It's natural for a man in this situation to see it as an opportunity for him to "prove" to *himself* he's a real man. As dating moves toward engagement, the answer to his question, *Am I a real man?* usually feels like a resounding, *Yes*.

Unfortunately, after the ring goes on and real life takes over, that can change. Without any ill will on the part of the wife, he may feel that her "helpful" criticisms are more numerous than her affirmations. The fear of inadequacy—*I'm not adequate as a man*—can creep into our minds, resulting in confusion, anger, and other problematic behaviors, like addictions or buying unneeded boy toys.[4]

HOPE FOR THE HUNGRY

So, how can we counter these challenging influences? Three things are necessary.

First, identify if father hunger is impacting you and in what ways. Remember, we can acknowledge a negative impact without bashing our parents.

Second, accept that even though our behaviors may be understandable as a result of our experiences, this does not justify them. We are still accountable to God and to others we may have hurt by our bad behavior.

Third, it is crucial to focus on God's view of what it means to be a man. Search the Scriptures for the characteristics of men that are important to God. One powerful verse is Ephesians 2:10. It says, "For we are his workmanship, created in Christ Jesus for good works, which God prepared beforehand, that we should walk in them" (ESV).

If you are a man, you are God's workmanship, His *masterpiece*, His handiwork. We are enough just as God makes us and as we do our best to walk in His ways. That is how God sees you because that is who you are. As you read these words, you are the exact image of *male* God wanted you to be—warts and all.

You don't need to depend on affirmation from the media, other people, or even the person you're marrying. God loves you as you are. But He'll work with you to become more like His Son, the ultimate man, Jesus, every day. And the side benefit? You will continue becoming the spouse your partner deserves.

QUESTIONS FOR HIM

1. In your life, do you feel the question, Am I a real man? was answered, distorted, or not answered? In what ways?
2. Describe any concerns you have about being the "man" your fiancée is looking for due to the lack of a solid model. Explain why you have these concerns. What do you think you are missing?

CHAPTER 5

How Father Hunger Can Impact Women

I finally understand that it's not a question of whether to have hope, but rather where, and with whom, you choose to lay your hope.[1]

—Cindy M. Birch, *He Never Came Home*

once encountered a young lady whose father left when she was a toddler. Other than the occasional picture she found or the stray, usually negative, comment from her mother, she had no conception of him. But just after her fifteenth birthday, her online searches finally produced a credible thread. Weeks later the heart that yearned for the man she was too young to remember would fulfill its quest. The meeting was set.

The thing that amazed me about this young lady was the depth of her drive to meet her dad—a dad she didn't know. But like a moth drawn to a flame, the desire to meet this man—her father—was powerful.

A father's absence, for whatever amount of time, often impacts ladies differently than men. As referenced in Tom Rodgers and Beverly Rodgers' book *Adult Children of Divorced Parents*, Dr. Neil Kalter explains one reason why:

> Children often see divorce as a form of rejection. . . . [and] young girls experience the emotional loss of [a] father. The continued limited involvement from the father is experienced as ongoing rejection by him. Many girls attribute this rejection to not being pretty enough or smart enough to please their father and engage him in regular frequent contacts. This causes intensified separation anxiety, denial, and avoidance of feelings associated with loss of father and object hunger for males.[2]

When I first started researching these issues and reviewed the evidence, I presumed that the findings were the exception—women on the extreme left and right sides of the chart in chapter 1. But I was mistaken. In twenty-plus years of working with adult children of divorce, I've found that these tendencies are far more common than any of us would like to admit.

I've also learned just how important the father is. Gaspard and Clifford write,

> A girl's relationship with her father is key to her femininity, sexuality, and identity as a woman. . . . Fathers serve as a crucial buffer because girls naturally tend to distance themselves from their mothers during adolescence. Unfortunately, girls who don't have this buffer may seek approval from boys and young men who are unavailable or wrong for them.[3]

I've seen this in my counseling office. You've probably seen it with others too. Perhaps this describes some of your life's journey.

Gaspard and Clifford sum up the hard truth regarding the significant result of father hunger by stating that after her parents' divorce, "Daughters may initially . . . doubt their own ability to find love and happiness in the future."[4] I would add that this doubt may linger, *even if they've found it.*

This is rooted, in great part, in not finding a safe and soothing answer to two questions that burn in the hearts of most girls and women: Am I beautiful? and Am I special? In this case, *beauty* is not the supermodel beauty you see on TV and social media. The deep longing of a girl's heart is to be beautiful in the eyes of her father. Kevin Leman, author of *What a Difference a Daddy Makes,* writes, "A daughter should never feel 'average' when she sees her reflection in her daddy's eyes." He later adds, "Young women need masculine approval that is freely given, not earned."[5]

Unfortunately, too often girls find the *yes* answers they crave from guys who attach strings to their feedback. "Yes," if you do this or that. Girls, and the women they become, often do what they feel is necessary to get this yes. Proverbs 27:7 explains why: "A person who is full refuses honey, but even bitter food tastes sweet to the hungry."

FATHER HUNGER FALLOUT WOMEN MAY EXPERIENCE

Without realizing their behavior is related to father hunger, women may become very sexually active in dating and relationships. However, when some of these ladies connect the dots, they experience guilt or shame. If that's you, it's important to know this: "If we confess our sins, he [God] is faithful and just and will forgive us our sins and purify us from all unrighteousness" (1 John 1:9 NIV). God loves us. God forgives us. God cares for us. Healing starts with Him, and there's nothing you've done that can negate these truths!

Confess what concerns you and pray to God right now, accepting His forgiveness. Psalm 103:13–14 states, "As a father has compassion on his children, so the LORD has compassion on those who fear Him; for He knows how we are formed, He remembers that we are dust" (NIV). When you ask for God's forgiveness, He pours out His compassion on you.

Also, depending on the nature of the behaviors you regret, consider seeking the help of a faith-based professional counselor with experience in those areas. Shame, remorse, and guilt can cause us to want to hide or isolate, but reaching out to a trusted source is a far better choice.

It's also possible that someone took advantage of your vulnerability against your will. It may have been a date, teacher, relative, boss, friend, or someone else. Some men can smell vulnerability, and they may have assaulted you. Here are some important helps:

Recognize that, regardless of the circumstances, the sexual abuse or rape was wrong. It shouldn't have happened, and it was not your fault. You don't have to carry the blame for someone else's abusive behavior.

Tell somebody about the abuse. Find someone who is equipped to help you through the recovery process. This is important because it *will* affect your marriage, and it's unfair for you to carry this burden alone.

Learn about the impact of sexual abuse. One good resource is June Hunt's book *How to Rise Above Abuse: Victory for Victims of Five Types of Abuse.*

Push aside the fear of dealing with abuse. You might think, *Kent, I have a wedding approaching. Do you really expect me to* *tell my fiancé now? What if he rejects me and calls off the wedding?* Your fear is understandable. This is a traumatic topic. This is why working with someone trained to address this type of issue is crucial. They can help you, and help you tell your fiancé should you feel led to do so.

Remember, God created sexual intimacy for marriage. Past sexual abuse can produce triggers, some long-buried, that can negatively impact this area of your marriage. Be bold, and do what is necessary to enjoy what God created for you two, without any hindrances.

HOPE FOR THE HUNGRY

I hope you see why father hunger is such an important issue to face and deal with.

Future brides, I encourage you to learn more about father hunger and where your vulnerabilities might lie. Use the Resources section at the back of this book, and spend time discovering how the issue has impacted your life. Carve out time for personal reflection. Seek assistance with a therapist, if necessary. Seeking godly professional counsel can also help you assess if it's possible and safe to take steps toward a relationship or stronger relationship with your father.

The most important step you can take is to pursue a strong relationship with your Heavenly Father. Psalm 10:14 says about

God, "The helpless commits himself to You; You are the helper of the fatherless" (NKJV). When you spend time in prayer and reading the Bible, God's Holy Spirit can open your eyes to the tender places in your heart. And that gives you the opportunity to challenge any lies you may expose with God's truth.

Future grooms, make it a priority to know about any father hunger symptoms your fiancée may be struggling with. Discover her vulnerabilities and determine how you can help. Remember the importance of reassuring her that she's beautiful to you inside and outside, and, after the wedding, that she is special to you inside and outside of the bedroom.

Take this to heart—you can't reassure her too much! Daily assurance—without her asking for it—is the goal. One-time or sporadic affirmations won't build the loving support base she needs.

WHAT MATTERS MOST

As we continue to consider the impact of father hunger, the most important thing to grasp is God's perspective on us.

Psalm 139:17–8 reads, "How precious are Your thoughts about me, O God! They are innumerable! I can't even count them" (NLT 1996). The Hebrew word for precious is *yaqar*, which means "to esteem, to be prized, to be valuable, to be precious, to be costly, rare."[6]

That is God's view of you—regardless of the past—men and ladies. And that's the view God wants you to have of yourself . . . because it's true. You have a Heavenly Father who knows *you* are precious.

It is important for you both to be aware of any father hunger issues that exist so you can support each other, avoid potential triggers, and assist each other in the healing process.

QUESTIONS FOR HER

1. Which father hunger issues in this chapter did you most relate to? Why?
2. In what ways have you received positive or negative answers to the questions, Am I beautiful? and Am I special?
3. How did you feel when you read about how precious you are to God?

Complications from Cohabitation

Husbands, love your wives, just as Christ loved the church and gave himself up for her.

Eph. 5:25 NIV

Wives, submit yourselves to your own husbands as you do to the Lord.

Eph. 5:22 NIV

Five years of prayers had been answered for Josh and Sarah. Chris had finally proposed to their daughter, Jasmine. While largely supportive of the couple, they'd made it clear they weren't happy with Jasmine living with someone unmarried. As people of faith, their daughter's arrangement was a source of awkward interactions and embarrassment among friends. But that was coming to an end, and they were ecstatic. But should they be?

According to Bowling Green State University researchers, "The vast majority of married couples lived with a cohabiting partner prior to marriage. Three-quarters (76%) of recent marriages (2015-2019) were preceded by cohabitation."[1] Through the years, the stigma of living together has decreased.

Cohabitation, shacking up, setting up house together, living in sin, or whatever the latest phrase is runs counter to most religious teachings, so it's natural that parents may feel relief and thankfulness for their children when a cohabiting arrangement ends. But research indicates that enthusiasm is only warranted under certain conditions.

One important consideration is whether the couple makes a conscious and joint decision to get married or simply slide into the marriage. In other words, marriage may seem like the next logical step, so inertia takes them down the aisle—whether they are compatible or not.

Dr. Teresa DiDonato notes, "Once people cohabitate, it's harder to break up, even if partners are not especially well-suited for each other. When momentum points to marriage, it can be hard to press the brakes."[2]

Exploring this further, researchers Manning and Cohen from Bowling Green University found that "the experience of cohabitation leads to increased acceptance of divorce and individuals in longer lasting cohabiting unions have even less positive attitudes toward family formation, marriage and childbearing."[3]

Glenn Stanton, a leading spokesperson in support of marriage and family, writes, "Couples who cohabit before marriage tend to exhibit more negative and less successful problem-solving skills than married couples."[4] He cites other research warning that "spouses who cohabit before marriage are less effective in soliciting support from their mate and less likely to be able to provide it themselves."[5]

These are vital issues to consider when planning together to build a strong marriage. However, gender differences also must be considered.

Terry Gaspard cites research by Dr. John Curtis showing that "the fundamental difference between men and woman . . . is that many women view living together as a step towards marriage while many men see it as a test drive."[6]

And for men, the "test drive" is beneficial most of the time. Domestic and international research shows that when a man is living with a woman he cleans less, cooks less, does less laundry,[7,8] and has "a convenient sex partner."[9] So why would he want a change? And that's where *sliding* comes in.

For five years Josh and Sarah's daughter, Jasmine, has hinted to Chris about marriage—particularly the past few years as her fertility clock's been ticking louder. Jasmine's mom has hinted about grandkids, but *not until marriage*. Jasmine was quiet for days after the last family reunion where she learned two of her younger cousins were getting married.

With pressure mounting, Chris cried "uncle" inside and bought a ring. Everybody was happy . . . except him. And, too often, sliding into marriage means stumbling into divorce a few years later.

So, Chris has proposed. Should Jasmine's parents (and Jasmine) have been happy or cautious? Very cautious. While couples who live together after engagement have significantly lower divorce rates than those who cohabited before this, in addition to the issues I and many others have raised, Stanton reports, "Cohabitors who live with a few different partners, then finally marry, face double the odds of divorce of those who cohabited only with their spouse."[10]

If a couple lives together before or after the engagement, it is very important that these issues are addressed prior to the nuptials, with the goal of creating a healthy marriage to avoid divorce. Sometimes that means avoiding a marriage, if it's for the wrong reasons.

In closing this difficult chapter, I want to avoid the risk of being misconstrued, and state that I don't condone living together for many reasons, including that the Bible is very clear about fornication—or having sex outside of marriage.[11] As 1 Corinthians 6:18 says, "Flee from sexual immorality. All other sins a person commits are outside the body, but whoever sins sexually, sins against their own body" (NIV).

Too often I've seen and heard of young women who live with a guy and give their all to him for six, eight, or more of their datable years, only to find out he isn't interested in anything more than sex. They're left with a poorer self-image, less time to find the husband they desire, and more pressure to beat the fertility clock. Worse, they can feel they've blown it with God (not true!) and stay away from God, who is the one true source of love for them.

However, this chapter is not about judgment. It's about acknowledging the facts and moving forward in a healthy way.

QUESTIONS

1. If you're living with your partner now, how and why was the decision made? Did you slide into living together, or did you both discuss that it was a step toward marriage?

2. Would you make the same choice to live together if you could go back and start again? (This is important! If you were guilted or pressured into the decision, it's likely that type of pressure will occur with other issues in the marriage. A therapist may be helpful to work through this.)

3. Are you getting married because you can't see yourself without your partner for the rest of your life, or because it just seems like the next step?

CHAPTER 7

Asking Questions and Discovering Answers Together

I still wonder, if I ever have children, Will their grandparents be able to sit together in the same room?[1]

—Jen Abbas, *Generation EX*

At the beginning of this book, we met an adult named Jamie with divorced parents. First, she was asking the wedding planner if her mother had to sit at the front. Then, at her premarital counseling class, she wondered how her fiancé, Garrison, could enter the circus of a family she belonged to.

Jamie's family background serves as a trigger factory that may affect Garrison in various and surprising ways. For example, he won't know that mistrust (because of her father's affair) is at the root of her outburst when he's unexpectedly late from work, unless this is discussed. This is why asking questions that rarely come up in premarital counseling sessions is necessary.

How we process these questions is important, but with whom we process them is just as important. Some individuals may want to do this by themselves. Others may want a friend to help. Because you're embarking on a life together, working through the questions together can be very helpful; however, I encourage you to also do this with someone trained to help you explore the answers in a healthy way.

Jamie is *subconsciously* scared to death Garrison will leave her. However, she's probably unaware of that submerged fear. Consequently, she may unconsciously test him or try to control him because of that lingering insecurity. A groom who has experienced parental infidelity may become jealous or controlling.

As we discussed in chapter 3, fear of abandonment and feelings of inadequacy can feed anger. These can appear as snide comments, quick-tempered responses, or explosive anger, for example. Fear of conflict can contribute to withdrawing and avoidant behaviors. So, for the fiancée and fiancé, addressing areas like this is important:

- How did you find out about your parent's affair?
- Were you asked to keep it a secret?
- What did your parent tell you about the affair?
- Did your parent share their feelings with you?
- Did the other parent share their feelings?

- What happened after the revelation of the affair? (Review the timeline of events.)
- What emotions do you experience regarding your parent's infidelity? What are your thoughts about men/women in general?
- With the freedom to be completely honest, do you fear your significant other might cheat on you?

I've only addressed infidelity with these questions because of its far-reaching negative impact—particularly on the foundational need for trust in a relationship. But couples with divorced parents who are engaged need to ask a variety of questions on a number of topics.

Gary Neuman, in his book *The Long Way Home: The Powerful 4-Step Plan for Adult Children of Divorce*, offers a list of some. As a child, were you . . .

- Nurtured?
- Shown physical demonstrations of love?
- Verbally told loving messages?
- Told "I love you" (How often?)
- Made to feel protected?
- Listened to? (Did my parents "get" me?)
- Encouraged to share your voice—your feelings, thoughts, and opinions?
- Celebrated?

- Happy?
- Dealt with honestly?
- Taught in a loving manner?[2]

These questions may seem unimportant or even trivial—which I would debate since even couples from intact families could benefit from them—but with parental divorce, the answers may reveal how often-unspoken expectations for the marriage relationship will be handled.

But those are the easy questions. Neuman's next set of questions involve pivotal considerations for adult children of divorce, which can have deeper negative influences on the marriage relationship. First, what was it like . . .

- Finding out about your parents' separation or divorce?
- Experiencing one parent leaving?
- Missing the parent who left?
- Going back and forth between parents?
- Hearing negative things about one parent from the other?

Did you find yourself . . .

- Being a messenger between parents?
- Being asked to spy on one parent for the other?
- Having to keep secrets from a parent?

How did you experience . . .

- Dealing with a parent's new boyfriend or girlfriend?
- Dealing with a stepparent?
- Dealing with stepsiblings?

How would you describe . . .

- How your parents managed school events?
- How your parents celebrated your birthday?
- Learning about child support?
- Worrying about family finances?
- Discovering or being told that one parent was unfaithful?[3]

If the future bride or groom's parents divorced after they were grown (a gray divorce), the following issues also apply:

- In what ways have your parents changed since the divorce?
- What are positive changes that have occurred since the divorce? Negative changes?
- What, if any, changes have occurred between you and your siblings? How have these changes affected you?
- What are your top three concerns related to the divorce?
- What are the top three aggravations you're experiencing with the divorce?

Going through a list like this accomplishes two things. First, it generates important personal insights that rarely come up naturally. Second, it helps identify the most important and impactful events and challenges, so any negative affect on the couple's relationship can be addressed and minimized.

For example, "Are you a spender or saver?" is different than asking, "Do you worry about having enough money to meet your needs?" The decrease in available funds after divorce is well-documented. Will your fiancé unknowingly overcompensate for insecurity in this area by overspending? Or will they compulsively save to ensure, "My kids will never be without like I was!"? Knowing this can help the other spouse avoid responding with criticism, and instead, process with their partner about the financial fear with understanding and compassion.

For adults with divorced parents, these nuanced questions are as important as the questions every couple needs to ask, such as, "How many kids to you want?" Or, "What are your expectations for the distribution of household duties?" And who decides what about sex?

It's also important to understand that a *justified reason* for the parents' divorce doesn't negate the necessity of working through these issues if you hope for a healthy relationship. An affair, abuse in the home, neglect, abandonment, substance abuse, or other situations may *explain* their divorce, but it's still important to process the cognitive, emotional, and spiritual impact of the related events. Doing this benefits both members of the couple since it decreases the likelihood of doing or saying things that may result in a negative response from your partner.

THE IMPACT OF SEXUAL HISTORY

If it hasn't been addressed prior to premarital counseling, a discussion about the couple's individual sexual history needs to take place—ideally with a neutral party like a counselor. It's common for children of divorce (particularly females) to have sex at earlier ages and with more partners.[4] By reviewing sexual history, I'm not talking about taking the covers off all the gruesome details. I'm referring to the number of sexual partners a person has engaged with, how recently, and if there are any lingering emotional attachments. Why? As a counselor, I've seen the problems that these attachments from the past can create later.

Additionally, multiple partners can distort our perspective of God's intention for the sacredness and beauty of sexual intimacy between a husband and wife. Virgins and individuals with only one partner prior to marriage (usually the eventual spouse) have the lowest divorce rates based on a variety of research. Two or more partners can significantly increase the likelihood of divorce.[5]

The good news is, "It appears that the risks of sexual experimentation before marriage can be overcome when one adopts beliefs and behaviors that foster enduring marriages."[6] This is why a biblical study of sexuality is a vital addition to premarital counseling with adult children of divorce. One great resource is clinical psychologist Juli Slattery's website, authenticintimacy.com.

An even more uncomfortable but related topic should be addressed between the bride-to-be and another female leader one-on-one. Have there been any abortions? Together, they can decide if an abortion-recovery program would be helpful. Abortions can affect women in different ways. For some, there appears to be little or no cognitive or emotional impact. For others, guilt, shame, anger, grief, anxiety, depression, spiritual confusion, and other emotions can linger long after the abortion.[7,8] Most women who've had an abortion fall somewhere in between these two experiences.

For some men, the abortion topic can be personal also. Perhaps they are the one that pushed for the abortion. Or maybe they didn't want the abortion, but the girl had the procedure anyway. In either case, processing through the related emotions (e.g., guilt, regret, unforgiveness) can be helpful and freeing. "The Lord is near to the brokenhearted and saves the crushed in spirit" (Psalm 34:18).

BEWARE OF THE HIDDEN OBVIOUS

In conclusion, I've heard the expression, "Satan does everything he can to get people into the bedroom before marriage, and everything he can to keep them out of the bedroom after the marriage occurs." The thought of not wanting to be intimate with your partner after marriage may seem absurd during the engagement, but with unspoken sexual baggage, trust me, it's not.

Because the sexual component of marriage is so important to couples, it's crucial to address any uncomfortable issues now so discord, unhappiness, and marital distress can be minimized later.

Another important consideration: A desire to avoid a question listed in this chapter could signal it as one that really needs to be addressed. We talked in chapter 3 about the fear of abandonment and fear of conflict. I encourage you to name and pray about any fear you're experiencing with this chapter. Isaiah 41:10 says, "Don't be afraid, for I am with you. Don't be discouraged, for I am your God. I will strengthen you and help you."

With God's help, press through your fear and have courageous conversations that can strengthen the foundation of your upcoming marriage.

QUESTIONS

1. Do you feel it's important to explore the types of questions in this chapter? Explain why or why not.
2. Do you have any concerns or fears over answering questions like those in this chapter? If yes, describe them.
3. Which questions create nervousness when you consider talking about them?

CHAPTER 8

What Is Your Image of a Family?

Think of children from families with loving, married parents as receiving a roadmap about love that, while not perfect, at least gives generally reliable directions toward the desired destination. In contrast, adult children of divorce are given a roadmap with whole sections missing, scribbled out, or wrong, leading them to dead-ends.[1]

—Daniel and Bethany Meola, *Life-Giving Wounds*

One of the great things about the Bible is that it shows real people with real families in real-life situations. One of those people was a young man named Joseph. Keep in mind that some of the cultural norms in the Old Testament, such as polygamy, don't apply today, but the principles do.

Genesis 37:2 tells us that Joseph was in a blended family, by today's definition. "He worked for his half brothers, the sons of his father's wives Bilhah and Zilpah." Another window into his step-family dynamics occurs in verses 3 and 4. "Now Israel [Jacob] loved Joseph more than any other of his sons, because he was the son of his old age. And he made him a robe of many colors. But when his brothers saw that their father loved him more than all his brothers, they hated him and could not speak peacefully to him" (ESV).

We learn that Joseph had half brothers, was favored by his father, and his brothers hated him. We also know something else about Joseph's household. His father had two more wives named Rachel and Leah. Genesis 29:30 tells us Jacob "loved Rachel more than Leah" (ESV). In verse 33, Leah indicates she knew this, saying, "Because the LORD has heard that I am hated, he has given me this son also" (ESV). That son was one of Joseph's older stepbrothers. But the point is, Leah believed she was hated by her husband, Jacob.

This "stepfamily" included twelve brothers, one sister, and four moms. Some of you reading this may think, *Four moms!?* But I'm reminded of my three moms (one biological and two stepmothers). Many of you understand the multiple-mom or multiple-dad thing. "I have a family bush instead of a family tree,"[2] author and ACD Jen Abbas commented in an interview.

That "family bush" can be tough sometimes. Perhaps you've also experienced what it's like when a father, mother, stepfather, or stepmother favored others more than you. Or maybe you relate to stepsiblings not liking you, isolating you, or mistreating you.

It's also possible this is all foreign to you. Short of what you've seen on a reality program, Joseph's stepfamily dynamics are beyond comprehension when compared to your (not perfect but) relatively stable, "normal," and loving family. But if you're marrying an ACD, this may be a window into their world. A world that will be combining with yours.

Ron Deal, founder of The Smart Stepfamily organization, cites research presenting sixty-seven variations of blended families. *Sixty-seven.*[3] For example, one version might include a stepmom and father, but an uninvolved birth mom. Another might contain three involved stepmothers and a mother. Which version does your loved one have? What dynamics is your future spouse used to or maybe trying to avoid?

These variations can be complicated, according to research cited in Constance Ahrons' book *The Good Divorce*. In it, she summarizes four types of divorced couples she discovered in her research. *Perfect Pals* were good friends after the divorce and included about 12 percent of couples in the study. *Cooperative Colleagues* (about 38 percent) had a decent, but not perfect, handle on the importance of good co-parenting for the kids' sake. *Angry Associates* included parents who argued a lot and maintained an antagonistic relationship. They constituted about 25 percent of the couples. *Fiery Foes* also came in at 25 percent, and included those who could barely talk without a lawyer.[4]

For children, these family types can become more complicated with the addition of girlfriends, boyfriends, partners, stepparents, other parties, and all their family associations.

Jen Abbas quoted "Bob" in her book *Generation EX: Adult Children of Divorce and the Healing of Our Pain,* who shared, "I hated my stepmom because she was the one who broke up my family. And yet I had to visit and eat turkey and mashed potatoes with her and always treat her as if she were an old friend of the family."[5]

Stephanie Staal, author of *The Love They Lost,* shared her similar experience in writing, "We were all comfortable with the extremely uncomfortable situation."[6] For those who experience these situations, *family* can have a very distorted image.

Another challenge to that image is what Dr. Daniel Meola refers to as "Emotional Homelessness." In the book *Life-Giving Wounds,* he and his wife, Bethany, write about the many transitions adult children of divorce experience:

All of these transitions and losses can lead to a sense of emotional homelessness, the feeling that children of divorce have of not quite fitting into either their father's or mother's new worlds. They don't feel at home in either because neither is the united home of their origin."[7]

Prior to the divorce, warts and all, *home* and *family* were synonymous. But after a divorce, our model of family-ness becomes incomplete, distorted, or absent. Troubling news indeed. However, if this is you, it reflects your past! It doesn't have to mold your future.

CHOOSING A BETTER PATH

Regardless of what type of family you experienced as a child, you can make the choice, today, to build a healthy marriage and family. Here are some suggestions to help.

Identify the image of a family you experienced. Reflect on what you've read in this chapter and do an honest assessment of both your family and your partner's family. What worked? What didn't work? Remember, no family is perfect.

Identify the image you want for your family. What would you like to change? What family ingredients are important to you? Which do you want to avoid?

Identify best practices that can help you create the family you envision. Don't hesitate to draw on the experiences of others.

Jack and Judith Balswick, authors of *The Family,* write, "Family relationships, as designed by God, are meant to be lived out in an atmosphere of grace and not law. Family life based upon covenant leads to an atmosphere of grace and forgiveness."[8] Grace and forgiveness strengthen the foundation of a healthy family.

In addition to these, other qualities of healthy marriages and families are shared in Focus on the Family's book (written by Jim Daly) *Why Family Matters*. These include: seeing the big picture, commitment, high regard, flexibility and grace, balance, joy and humor, and a service mindset.[9]

Let's break these down.

1. ***Seeing the big picture***—Healthy families see the meaning of family as bigger than themselves. The family exists to bring glory to God.

2. ***Commitment***—Family members are committed for the long haul. As God is covenanted (unshakably committed) to His children, we are to be in covenant with each other as spouses and family members.

3. ***High regard***—Respect, honor, care, and concern are essential ingredients for a healthy family environment.

4. ***Flexibility and grace***—I recall a pastor saying, "Blessed are the flexible, for they shall not be broken." I would add, "and they will not break each other."

5. ***Balance***—Grace, boundaries, and forgiveness are equal parts of the three-legged stool that supports the family. If any one of them falters, things move out of balance.

6. ***Joy and humor***—A family that laughs together stays together.

7. ***A service mindset***—Jesus said, "For even the Son of Man came not to be served but to serve others and to

give his life as a ransom for many" (Matthew 20:28). In marriage and family, a heart of serving each other honors God and creates an atmosphere of humility and mercy.

These qualities are often covered in biblical premarital counseling; however, it's important to remember that the issues parental divorce tends to produce often undermine them. This is true in part due to a fractured picture of the family, when individuals became more important than the whole. Commitment stopped. Criticism, contempt, and dishonor often replaced high regard. Unforgiveness and bitterness supplanted flexibility and grace.

Balance became imbalance as the marital relationship changed from the biblical call Jesus gave: "'The two shall become one flesh'; so, then they are no longer two, but one flesh" (Mark 10:8 NKJV). Instead, it became two individuals with individual lifestyles, absent the compromise that oneness necessitates. Self-preservation replaced a heart of service.

I remind you that my intent is not to dishonor parents. Often, one parent had the divorce thrust on them from the other. But it's important to identify the areas of challenge that affect you or your loved one so they can be addressed and remedied as much as possible. New tools need to be incorporated into building the clear and healthy family you long for.

QUESTIONS

1. Is your experience of family mostly positive, negative, or neutral? Explain why.
2. What concerns do you have about creating your own healthy family?
3. What practical steps can you and your significant other implement to achieve your goal of building a loving family?

CHAPTER 9

Communication Pitfalls of Adults with Divorced Parents

*With the tongue we praise our Lord and Father, and with it
we curse human beings, who have been made in God's likeness.
Out of the same mouth come praise and cursing. My brothers
and sisters, this should not be.*

James 3:9–10 NIV

As Antonio and his fiancée, Alisa, watched a video titled "5
Steps for Great Marital Communication" on her phone,
he thought about the five steps of marital communication he'd
experienced for the first fourteen years of his life. They included
screaming, sarcasm, suspicion, scorn, and sobbing. The psychologist in the video was sharing concepts for which Antonio had
no frame of reference.

Couple communication is covered in most marriage workshops, teachings, and marital or premarital counseling sessions. This is often one of the top concerns couples have when they come to me for marital counseling—their inability to engage in constructive communication and resolve conflict.

For those with divorced parents, marital communication is an interesting game, as their primary model for it comes typically from their parents. In many cases, this wasn't great. But once a couple is engaged, they'll soon be taking these limited and often contorted skills into their marriage.

In this chapter we'll look at two (of the many) issues adults with divorced parents can struggle with in relational communication: fear and secret-keeping.

FEAR AND COMMUNICATION

In chapter 1, the first issues I listed that impact adults with divorced parents were anger and fear, including fears of conflict, abandonment, being inadequate or inferior, doom, and divorce. I include anger with fear here because of the anger-fear connection.

In their book *Adult Children of Divorced Parents*, Beverly and Tom Rodgers break down anger triggers into the acronym GIFT: Guilt, Inferiority/Inadequacy, Fear, and Trauma (or pain). These primary feelings can create anger. The authors write that it's better "to discuss the root rather than the rage."[1]

The root for adult children of divorce is often fear, and unaddressed fear can create an anger-fear communication cycle that weakens marriages. Here's an illustration.

Fear is fueling this cycle. You may want to review the fear section in chapter 1 to refresh yourself on any fears you may be vulnerable to.

Another misbelief common to adult children of divorce is the fear that any conflict can lead to divorce. For people from intact homes, this assumption makes no sense. *Conflict is normal. It doesn't mean the end of the world!* But it felt like the end of the world for your partner when his or her parents divorced. There was lots of conflict. The end was divorce. So, the natural and subconscious conclusion of someone six, twelve, or sixteen years old is that conflict leads to divorce.

Further strengthening this premise is the likelihood that your ACD partner has experienced relationships that ended after conflict. For example, a nineteen-year-old lacks effective conflict-resolution skills and carries fear from parental divorce. This fear feeds relational conflict and will likely lead to a breakup, reinforcing the originally programmed belief that conflict *causes* relationships to end. We become inwardly terrified it will happen in our marriage.

So, it's vital to expose this distortion and program our minds with the truth. As Jack and Judith Balswick write in *The Family*, "Conflict is to be expected when two distinct and unique individuals express themselves equally. Marriage without conflict often signifies that one partner has given up personhood."[2] People that give up their personhood (become conflict avoidant) eventually resent it, get upset, and the cycle illustrated in the previous diagram fires up.

Fear can interfere with healthy communication by keeping us from asking for what we really want. Maybe you're thinking, *I'd much rather go to the Italian restaurant,* but you go to the Greek restaurant because you don't want to upset your fiancée. This may be true even though, if she knew how you felt, she'd gladly go to the Italian restaurant.

Fear-based communication often creates miscommunication, because some facts of a situation remain hidden. To help couples in counseling avoid this, I teach them how to ask clarifying questions. These are necessary because we don't always say what we mean, or all that we mean. For example, one person may say, "That was the worst thing you could have said." You might be tempted to hear those words and conclude that you've blown the whole relationship. When fear kicks in, it's all too easy to catastrophize. But a healthier response might be, "I can see you're upset. Please tell me why this was the worst thing I could have said." This calmer response is more likely to elicit an answer like one of these:

- Because it reminded me of a mistake I made that hurt a friend.
- Because I'm really tired, and I just couldn't handle that additional weight right now.
- Because I realized that I need to change my entire agenda now to make this schedule work.

Here's a question. Do any of those responses indicate that you're a rotten dog and never get anything right, so your partner will be leaving you? If we're not careful, as seen in this example, fears of inadequacy, abandonment, and doom can take our brains in a very unhealthy and often untrue direction.

Fear-based communication or lack of communication also rob us of relational intimacy. Fear limits trust and vulnerability, which are key to relationship bonding. For healthy communication to have a chance, our fear-tinted glasses must be removed.

SECRET-KEEPING IN COMMUNICATION

An unfortunate by-product of parental divorce can be the tendency to keep secrets. A seven-year-old knows that certain things you say about Dad make Mom upset and vice versa. The child also knows that what happens in the home stays in the home. Dirty laundry isn't to be shared with outsiders. The child learns to filter his or her communication and keeps secrets to themselves.

For the fiancée from an intact home, a secret is not telling Mom what Dad bought for her birthday. For the fiancée from a divorced home, the secret is not telling Dad that Mom has a new boyfriend. Or even something as simple as saying she enjoyed her vacation with Dad and his new wife. The cost of telling the truth could result in a sigh, a fake smile, tears, or not being allowed to go on vacations with "that woman" or "that loser" anymore—all of which strain a child's brain.

For those of you from intact families, it's important to grasp that your future spouse may fear the same reaction from you. Should you respond in one of those ways, even with a sigh, it confirms their subconscious belief that the truth is danger-ous. You and I understand this is not true, but it's probably in their mental programming. Awareness can help you extend grace, compassion, and reassurance if you become aware of any secret-keeping.

For the adult child of divorce, be aware that secret-keeping may be as normal as breathing for you because you've done it so long. Which raises another communication problem: lying.

We started this chapter talking about fear. Fear can feed secret-keeping and lead to lying as well. In the past, we may have lied to protect ourselves or others—a parent, a sibling, a step-relative. After a while, lying becomes normal and easy—almost automatic. But both lying and secret-keeping almost always have a detrimental impact on the marital relationship.

This poses an even more significant problem because Proverbs 6:17 says God hates a lying tongue. It is detestable to Him. If fear is leading you in this type of behavior, repent, accept forgiveness, and commit to speaking truth in love. Work hard to not lie or keep secrets (other than birthday gifts) due to fear.

This gives us the freedom to say how we really feel instead of burying our thoughts out of fear of upsetting things. We can say things like this:

- I'm hurting.
- I feel embarrassed when you say that.
- I'm tired of my parents not getting along whenever they're together.
- I'm angry because I'm feeling . . .
- I'd really prefer to go to the park.

Our experience or our fear taught us that what we say can hurt people, so we may keep our thoughts secret or tell lies. As children we had to pick and choose what to tell which parent, so we may think we can't tell our spouse something they may not want to hear. But when effective communication methods are used, this is usually not true.

OVERCOMING FEARS AND SECRET-KEEPING IN COMMUNICATION

In addition to identifying and addressing the tendency toward fear dominance and secret-keeping, these steps can help.

Accept the fact that your spouse is not one of your parents. In most cases, they can be upset with what we did or said *and* still love us and want to be with us. When clients struggle with this, I have them create a truth card, a 3x5 card that includes two or three written statements that are absolutely true to them. For those of faith, I'll have them add a scripture to this list, one they don't doubt is true *for them*. If you doubt, "I can do all things through Christ who me strengthens me" (Philippians 4:13 NKJV) because of a challenge you're facing, opt for another verse, such as Hebrews 13:6: "The Lord is my helper; I will not fear; what can man do to me?" (ESV). Truth cards help us reframe our distorted beliefs.

Learn effective communication skills. Most of us weren't taught these skills in school, and with divorced parents, we didn't see effective communication skills modeled at home. But there are many tools and methods you can learn and apply to communicate without the fear of blowing up the relationship.

Identify, pray for, and apply God's wisdom before you share your thoughts. The Bible says: "If you need wisdom, ask our generous God, and he will give it to you. He will not rebuke you for asking" (James 1:5).

Take this chapter to heart, and you'll be well on your way to avoiding the communication pitfalls that so many adult children of divorce (and their loved ones) experience.

QUESTIONS

1. What fears do you think impact your communication with your future spouse?
2. How did secret-keeping play out in your childhood? How does it play out today?
3. Are you afraid to share with your partner what and how you really feel, or what you really want? Why or why not?

CHAPTER 10

Parenting Without a Clear Road Map

Parenting is like trying to nail Jell-O to the wall.

—Unknown author

Halen was steaming, and so was Mason.

Halen: How could you hit our child like that?!

Mason: I just tapped her on the back of the hand!

H: She's two. They say that sort of violence can scar them!

M: Violence?! I tapped her on the back of the hand. Once!

H: My parents never laid a hand on us and we grew up fine.

M: I wouldn't call your brother fine.

H: Well, at least they didn't beat us like your parents did.

M: My parents didn't beat us. They applied appropriate, loving discipline, and we are better people because of it!

H: You'll never understand!

M: Well, at least I'm not spoiled!

And on it goes. But here's a question. Who is right, Halen or Mason? The answer depends on your background. Conflicts over sex, handling money, and parenting styles are the main three categories that spur couples to seek counseling help.

Parenting styles are often a mix of influences, but heavily weighted by what we experienced in childhood. We assess and rate our parents' performance and throw out things we feel were ineffective, unnecessary, and inappropriate, or are currently unpopular.

Adults with divorced parents may struggle to identify positive parenting methods they'd like to repeat. Often, our memories are weighted toward the post-divorce period. During this time the parenting model may be incomplete or worse. For example, it's not uncommon for rules to be significantly different between Mom's and Dad's home after the divorce. There might be a late curfew in one house and an early curfew in the other. Eating dinner separately may be the norm in one home, but unacceptable in the other. Discipline can become erratic if there is any at all.

Busyness and guilt can also affect divorced parents' parenting style. Some parents back off of discipline, thinking, *The kids are already experiencing enough trauma.* Others are busy keeping a roof over everyone's head, and their parenting defaults to the best they can do with all their limitations; or, they may transfer the responsibility for discipline to the oldest child or oldest daughter.

The parenting model children of divorce observe can be further impacted by well-meaning stepparents who overstep their perceived authority too quickly. The stepfather or stepmother may feel that the biological parent is too soft on the kids and institute their own parenting methods. This can create a backlash among the kids and among adult children of divorce, who may develop a lenient style of parenting as a result.

When it comes to parenting preferences, differences are normal. For example, I see a difference in expectations when couples first become parents. New moms tend to assume dads have innate bonding desires and experience taking care of babies. Moms may forget that while they watched siblings and probably babysat in their younger years, their spouse likely didn't. So, the things moms think, *They should just know,* dads may not. Here is where it can get problematic.

Bringing a baby home can expose a dad's lack of training and feelings of inadequacy whether they come from intact or broken homes. But for dads with divorced parents, the fear of inadequacy can trigger the fear-anger model we discussed earlier. Without strong communication tools and awareness of these potential trouble areas, an already stressful time can be exacerbated.

As the kids get older, discipline comes to the forefront and disagreements like the one Mason and Halen experienced can occur. Questions arise, like, How do we handle a three-year-old's defiance? Or an eight-year-old throwing his toys across the room? Usually, for better or worse, our parents' model forms our basic template. We adjust that template by adding things we liked about their methods of parenting and deleting others. A dash of social media advice, a book or two, and some friend's input may round out our template.

Problems start when the new mom and dad realize they have different templates. Ideally, premarital counseling will have addressed this, but often it comes as a shock. For adult children of divorce, that shock can trigger many of the fears we've mentioned. But there are steps we can take to elevate our parenting.

BUILDING A NEW PARENTING TEMPLATE TOGETHER

Identify your current parenting template. Share your templates with each other. Discuss how you were raised. What you liked. What you didn't. Share things you would "never do" to your children. Also, accept that most people experienced at least some positive parenting skills from their parents before and after the divorce. Be careful of disregarding your parents' parenting experience altogether. You may be overlooking some positive characteristics you missed in your template.

***Remember the distinction between* wrong *versus* different.** Emerson Eggerich heads a ministry called *Love and Respect.* In it, he teaches how much of the conflict couples experience is driven by God-designed differences between men and women. The problem comes when we see the difference in a spouse as wrong.

With parenting, the same holds true. Letting a young child play alone in a busy street is wrong. How close the child is allowed to the street (with appropriate precautions) may be a difference of opinion. Most of what I see in my counseling office, where parenting is concerned, are differences based on individual templates, not matters that are inherently right or wrong.

Also, thinking the other is *wrong* leans us toward an us-or-them focus. *I'm right. You're wrong.* Having a *different* mindset presumes we both may be right or have parts of the truth. This tends toward an us-us focus, which is the goal. This view fosters a positive outlook and greatly increases the opportunity for creating solutions agreeable to both.

Avoid the perfection delusion. If we aren't careful, our desire to parent well when we think our parents did it wrong can move us toward an unhealthy expectation of perfect parenting. Pressure from social media and comparisons to other parents can feed this delusion. Kids wouldn't behave correctly all the time, or always make healthy decisions, even if we could parent without flaws, but we will not do everything perfectly. Only God is perfect.

In Genesis 2:22, we read about God (the perfect parent) and His two kids (Adam and Eve). "Then the LORD God made a woman from the rib he had taken out of the man, and he brought her to the man" (NIV). Genesis 3:6 shares how God's kids broke the only rule He'd given: Don't eat from the tree of the knowledge of good and evil. "When the woman saw that the fruit of the tree was good for food and pleasing to the eye, and also desirable for gaining wisdom, she took some and ate it. She also gave some to her husband, who was with her, and he ate it" (NIV).

In Genesis 3:12, God's "teenagers" accept responsibility for their actions—*not!* Adam said, "The woman you put here with me—she gave me some fruit from the tree, and I ate it" (NIV). In verse 23, God "grounds" Adam and Eve: "So the LORD God banished him from the Garden of Eden to work the ground from which he had been taken" (NIV).

Remember this when you feel inadequate or a failure as a parent. Even the perfect parent had children who rebelled. The best thing you can do for your kids is strengthen your marriage covenant daily. It won't be perfect, but your kids will be blessed by default. Here are some suggestions for this.

Find good resources. Good resources are biblical, real, and normal. Be careful of Facebook personas who have ten kids, two full-time jobs, great marriages, and perfect lives. They are the only ones—not the norm. Try Focus on the Family; they are a great source for parenting resources.

Remember, God is with you. The same God who banished Adam and Eve guided their lives till their deaths. He loved them, and He loves you. Through the power of His Son, Jesus, He will give you the strength to do this parenting thing well— and well together.

Enjoy the journey. I can't quote the source, but I once heard this saying: "With parenting the days are long, but the years are short." As a father of three adult kids, I can validate that statement. I look at pictures of our kids when they were young or as newborns and have no idea where the time went.

Parenting can be tough. Sometimes it may feel like you are parenting with one arm tied behind your back, but even as a child of divorce, the cycle can be broken when you take intentional steps to change course.

QUESTIONS

1. Describe the parenting you experienced growing up. Ask your partner what they experienced growing up.
2. What are the areas in which you feel inadequate regarding parenting (e.g., knowing what to say or do, disciplining the child, etc.)?
3. What resources will you access to help strengthen the areas of concern you listed?

CHAPTER 11

Building a Thriving Stepfamily

Stepfamilies, like machines, are subject to the complexity principle: the more working parts, the greater the risk of breakdown.[1]

—E. Mavis Hetherington, *For Better or for Worse*

Moura never thought she'd meet a decent guy—not with her six-year-old, Desman. Guys didn't want kids.

Tom had given up on finding anyone who could love his daughters as much as he did. How ironic that Moura and Tom would meet, not through friends or a dating service, but through their kids talking at the grocery store.

Tom and Moura learned that they had much in common. Both hadn't wanted their divorces. Both were slow to get back into the dating scene. Both had lost hope. And eventually, both were very happy and ready to build a new life together.

Unfortunately, I've noticed a disturbing trend among clients and others in stepfamilies. Couples like Moura and Tom, who enter stepfamilies, seem to get less premarital counseling than others. Not because they don't want it, but because somehow, because they've been married before, they feel they're okay. However, given the layers of complexities that come with stepfamilies, and the divorce(s) many of them launched from, I believe more counseling is necessary, not less.

Premarital counseling for stepfamily couples is also important because of the number of people involved. One study showed that up to 40 percent of new marriages include at least one partner who is remarrying. And around 20 percent of those include couples like Tom and Moura, who are both remarrying.[2] The majority of people I've encountered underestimated the struggles stepparents can face and *the stress that can put on their marriage.*

Stepfamilies often experience unique challenges, stressors, and emotions. In her book *In Their Shoes*, Lauren Reitsema shares this sentiment from a stepmom: "I've accepted that this will hurt a little bit, every day, forever."[3] Stepparents also can face feelings of rejection and inadequacy, fear of abandonment and conflict, and more. Do any of these sound familiar? Adult children of divorce also tend to be pre-disposed to these fears.

Believe it or not, I'm not trying to scare you away from marriage. There are tools that can guide you through the maze of being a couple in a blended family and stepparenting itself.

However, while I felt it very important to broach this topic, it requires far more attention than this book can devote to it. So, if you are creating a stepfamily, I encourage you to google "Ron Deal" and review the variety of solid, biblical resources his Smart Stepfamilies organization offers. Among other lessons, learning how a crockpot philosophy versus a blender or microwave philosophy can increase your chances of success is crucial before you walk down the aisle.

Proverbs 11:14 says, "Where there is no [wise, intelligent] guidance, the people fall [and go off course like a ship without a helm], but in the abundance of [wise and godly] counselors there is victory" (AMPC). This couldn't be truer when it comes to creating a successful stepfamily.

QUESTIONS

1. In what ways have you considered the impact of creating a blended family on celebrating holidays, deciding visitation schedules, combining kids, and more, while simultaneously learning about your new spouse?

2. What concerns do you have about blending your families?

3. Do one or both of you have one or more ex-spouses? How is your relationship with that ex or exes? What are the potential ways they could impact your new marriage?

CHAPTER 12

Getting Married with Divorced Parents in the Mix

The wedding of a bride or groom whose parents are divorced or separated is handled just as any first wedding would be, with a few special considerations. Seating, in particular, becomes a problem if relationships are strained. Things get even more convoluted when both the bride and the groom's parents are divorced.[1]

—Jann Blackstone-Ford and Sharyl Jupe,
Ex-Etiquette for Weddings

First, if you skipped to this chapter, gotcha! I don't blame you, but I really need you to go back to the beginning and work through the book. Here's why.

To process this chapter effectively, it's critical to work through the issues in the previous chapters. For example, it will be difficult to apply some of the boundaries we'll discuss if you haven't addressed your fear of conflict or anger issues. Weddings are emotional times. Weddings with divorced parents can be "I wish we'd eloped" times. But being aware of how our parents' divorce impacted us can enable us and our betrothed to work together to handle challenges more effectively.

Kent, we have four weeks until the wedding and we just found this book! Got it. It's a time crunch on steroids. Then prayerfully use this chapter *while* processing through the rest of the book. Remember, your goal is not to survive and get through the wedding. Your goal is to celebrate one of the most important days of your life and start a healthy and long-lasting marriage. Take the time to do this!

A FEW MILLION CONSIDERATIONS

Now, back to the epigraph at the beginning of this chapter, which mentioned "a few special considerations" for weddings involving divorced or separated parents. I would change "a few" to "a few *million*."

Remember in chapter 1 how Jamie asked the wedding coordinator if her mom had to sit in the front row? That's only question 1,486. Here's a sample of some others.

- Who is invited to the wedding and who isn't? Stepgrandparents? Stepsiblings? Ex-stepgrandparents? Ex-stepsiblings? Who decides?
- Where do relatives who may or may not get along sit?
- Who do *you* want in the pictures and in what groups? Do *you* want a picture with Mom and Dad together? (Be careful. Siblings may not even agree with this, but it's your wedding.)
- Who does the bride want to walk her down the aisle? To give her away? Start by answering this question honestly, not politically correctly, and work from there.
- What are the options if Mom and Dad don't get along? (I've heard of situations where the first time the parents were together in years was at the wedding rehearsal.)
- Who can toast?
- Will you have bridal dances? Which ones? Will the traditional daddy-daughter or mother-son dance work?

The ability to answer questions like these can be problematic because, for adults with divorced parents, the people who are usually most involved in the wedding (the parents), can be the source of your anxiety. But tackling these types of issues before the big event can greatly increase your ability to enjoy your wedding day.

PREPARING FOR YOUR WEDDING WHEN YOUR PARENTS HAVE DIVORCED

So, what to do? Here are six suggestions:

First, resist wrapping yourself in denial. Accept that this wedding is a big deal to you. It's likely that you have powerful feelings attached to it. You may also have strong feelings regarding your parents' possible stunts during the festivities—or those of their partners. Acknowledge them and process through them. You can bury these emotions and push through, but years of regret and resentment can result if you minimized or discounted your thoughts and didn't celebrate the event the way you'd liked.

Second, seek God's wisdom and strength throughout this process. Earlier I cited Philippians 4:6. "Do not be anxious about anything, but in every situation, by prayer and petition, with thanksgiving, present your requests to God" (NIV). If we're not careful, we can read that as a casual reminder to simply pray to God. But this was written during the first century. At this time, choosing to follow Christ could result, at best, in losing your family, your friends, your job, and your home. At worst, you could be jailed or killed. So, the apostle Paul's words were shared with people who had many reasons to be anxious. But he encouraged them to trust God.

The next verse says, "Then you will experience God's peace, which exceeds anything we can understand. His peace will guard your hearts and minds as you live in Christ Jesus" (v. 7).

Could you use some peace right now? Here's your choice: You can use *your* wisdom or God's, *your* strength or God's. You can grit your teeth and bear it or have joy and peace that seems impossible given what you face. Peace was possible for the first-century hearers of these words. It is possible for you too!

If, unlike those hearers in the first century, you don't have a personal relationship with Jesus, please see the section titled "An Invitation from Jesus" near the end of this book. It's the most important step you can take to prepare for your marriage and the years to follow.

Third, make sure you're processing through any ACD issues that affect you. Doing so is particularly important if you skipped to this chapter! This will equip you to make sound decisions without the influence of fear and anger.

Fourth, identify any wedding-related issues that create conflict in your mind. Process them with your partner and premarital leader, a counselor, your wedding coordinator, an objective friend, or another trusted source.

Fifth, avoid alienating your divorced parents in this process by gravitating to the "normal" and "calmness" of your future in-laws. If your future spouse comes from an intact family, you may be tempted to drift from the tension or chaos of your parents during this busy time and attach more to them. Another subtle challenge can be whether to accept advice from parents whose marriage didn't survive. Though their marriage may not have lasted, most parents care deeply about your event and can have constructive things to share.

Sixth, develop and communicate a plan that includes boundaries. For example, it's crucial, and just plain courteous, to let people know who is doing what and when. I've heard of situations where parents thought they were walking the bride down the aisle only to find out, at the rehearsal, this wasn't the case.

This plan should include responses to the questions listed earlier in this chapter and, if these solutions involve boundaries (and many will), review the discussion of boundaries in chapter 2.

This may seem overwhelming. And if we look at the whole picture instead of working through issues one at a time, it can be. But remember, you've taken a strong step toward managing various parts of planning for your wedding more effectively. Working through these issues can give you more control—not in a dictatorial sense, but in the authoritative and loving style that may be necessary to rein in the various people involved in this blessed event.

Be encouraged! You now have many choices, which is far better than simply surviving the wedding or eloping!

QUESTIONS

1. Are there concerns you haven't told your partner or premarital counseling leader about? Why?
2. Of the five wedding-preparation steps, which ones cause you the most concern? Why?
3. Which of those steps would be most helpful to talk about with your partner?

CHAPTER 13

A Hope-Filled Future

*A successful marriage requires falling in love many times—
always with the same person.*

—Mignon McLaughlin

Remember our composite couple, Jamie and Garrison, from chapter 1? Here is their update: During a call with the marriage coordinator, Jamie burst into tears because of the pressure she felt trying to manage her family's dynamics for the wedding. The coordinator mentioned a counselor friend familiar with children of divorce issues, and Jamie saw her.

Over the next year, including the first seven months of their marriage, Jamie met with the counselor. They processed through anger, mistrust, and Jamie's fears, including the fear that Garrison would leave her—like her father had left her mom. Garrison attended the counseling sessions during the last month and together they learned about forgiveness and boundaries.

On their first anniversary, they celebrated a deep love together. It wasn't free from lingering ACD challenges, but they were able to work through them with God's truth and the tools they'd learned. Jamie's intentional steps to address her issues and their trust in God have greatly decreased the likelihood of Garrison and Jamie becoming a statistic.

Are you encouraged? Overwhelmed? Both? Regardless of all that's been written to this point, nothing is as important as knowing that the institution of marriage was God's idea. We see this when the religious rulers challenged Jesus on divorce.

> And Pharisees came up to him and tested him by asking, "Is it lawful to divorce one's wife for any cause?" He answered, "Have you not read that he who created them from the beginning made them male and female, and said, 'Therefore a man shall leave his father and his mother and hold fast to his wife, and the two shall become one flesh'? So they are no longer two but one flesh. What therefore God has joined together, let not man separate." (Matthew 19:3–6 ESV)

Marriage was intended to last a lifetime, but that's not what many of us experienced with our parents. It's natural to have doubts when most of us have attended weddings where the bride and groom say I accept you "till death do us part," and it's the second or third time they've done so. And please remember that I'm not throwing stones. My father said the "till death" phrase three times.

But, with all due love, honor, and respect, I am not my father. And you are not your parents. And, most importantly, "If God is for us, who can ever be against us?" (Romans 8:1). In John 10:10 Jesus said, "The thief comes only to steal and kill and destroy. I came that they may have life and have it abundantly" (ESV). That includes an abundant marriage that is full of the joys and challenges that life can bring. And there *will* be challenges.

But you've taken a *huge* step toward beating the statistics and having a marriage that goes the distance. You've chosen to get information and resources that can help you accomplish the goals you're learning in the rest of your premarital counseling meetings. Now, instead of thinking, *That's true, but . . .* you can say with confidence, *That's true, and we can do this!*

However, having a strong marriage takes more than willpower and information. *The Marriage Masterpiece* workbook notes, "Our highest fulfillment in marriage comes when God is invited not only to be a part of the ceremony, but also to be the ever-present, all-sustaining strength of the relationship. . . . True happiness comes from the three-way relationship between a man, a woman, and God."[1]

I can vouch for that—and not because I had the perfect marriage. Statistically, my marriage to Kathy of more than forty years never should have made it. I had divorced parents, and Kathy was raised in a home where alcohol-related issues were a problem. We both dragged a suitcase full of issues down the aisle on our wedding day. Those issues, combined with virtually no marriage preparation, contributed to years of dysfunction.

I committed my life to Jesus, at least in word, four years after we married. Ten to fifteen years after our wedding, I submitted my life to Jesus. It was then I began seeing God guide me to helpful resources and a deeper understanding of the Bible. This strengthened His process of molding me into the husband Kathy deserved. God worked in both of our lives, and I now live the abundant life Jesus offers.

My prayer is that you embrace what you've learned as we've explored the possible ways your parents' divorce impacted you and could adversely affect your marriage.

The key verse of Adult Children of Divorce Ministries, 2 Corinthians 1:3–4, can also be the key verse for your healing. "Blessed be the God and Father of our Lord Jesus Christ, the Father of mercies and God of all comfort, who comforts us in all our affliction, so that we may be able to comfort those who are in any affliction, with the comfort with which we ourselves are comforted by God" (ESV).

I've received God's comfort and healing, so I share it with you. You can also receive God's comfort and healing and share it with others. Break the fear and cycle of divorce to enjoy a marriage that goes the distance, and help other adult children of divorce do likewise. The resource section of this book includes many sources with valuable information for this very purpose.

Now to Him who is able to do exceedingly abundantly above all that we ask or think, according to the power that works in us, to Him be glory in the church by Christ Jesus to all generations, forever and ever. Amen. (Ephesians 3:20–21 NKJV)

AN INVITATION FROM JESUS

To be fully equipped to succeed going forward, you need the Holy Spirit of God. He has the power to help you overcome the issues this book discusses. A person receives the Holy Spirit when he or she accepts Jesus Christ as their Lord. However, accepting Jesus is even more important for another reason.

Through Jesus Christ, you can have your sins forgiven—anything you've done wrong—and spend eternity with the one true God in heaven. The Bible is very clear: Those who have Jesus Christ have eternal life, and those who don't will stand (without Jesus) before God's wrath against the sin that is in them. Only Jesus can shield you from God's just punishment for your sins.

The Bible states, "Everyone has sinned" (Romans 3:23). It goes on to say that our sins earn us eternal separation from God. This means without Jesus, we won't be in heaven with God when we die. We will be in hell. Jesus said, "I am the way, and the truth, and the life. No one comes to the Father except through me" (John 14:6 ESV).

The good news is, "If you confess with your mouth that Jesus is Lord and believe in your heart that God raised him from the dead, you will be saved" (Rom. 10:9–10 ESV).

Jesus offers us forgiveness for our sins and healing from the hurts of this world, including issues we acquired from our parents' divorce.

To those who accept him as their Savior, Jesus offers forgiveness, the Holy Spirit, *and* "love, joy, peace, patience, kindness, goodness, faithfulness, gentleness, [and] self-control" (Gal. 5:22–23 ESV). Aren't these the very things you're seeking on your journey with this book?

Accept Jesus' offer to save you from your sins and to be your source of wisdom and strength today.

ACKNOWLEDGMENTS

To my beloved wife, Kathy, who hung with me through years of ACD issues. Thank you for your steadfast love and faith that I'd eventually become the husband you deserved.

Author Amber Lia selflessly and generously shared her wisdom and unknowingly motivated me to discipline myself and write this book. Thank you, Amber!

Janet Blakely, your tenacious editing has once again enabled me to provide a strong manuscript to professional editors Margot Starbuck and Kristin Spann from Edit Resource. Thank you, ladies. And additional thanks to Elisa Stanford and the rest of the Edit Resource team for your input and dedication to this work.

Thank you, Rebecca Darga and Jessica Todd, for taking time to explore the draft through the eyes of an ACD.

Thank you, Kimberly, for making sure this work was biblically and psychologically sound.

Thank you to the board members of Adults with Divorced Parents Ministries for your unwavering support.

Thank you to our prayer-warrior team. Your support in this effort was crucial.

Thank you to Arvid and Kris Wallen for their willingness to support this project with their skill and knowledge.

And a heartfelt thank-you to authors, counselors, and researchers, like the late Judith Wallerstein, who were willing to say the unpopular thing so people like us to could identify and heal from the real impact of our parents' divorce.

BIBLIOGRAPHY OF RESOURCES

Abbas, Jen. *Generation EX: Adult Children of Divorce and the Healing of Our Pain.* WaterBrook Press, 2004.

Darcie, Kent, *Choose a Better Path: Overcoming the Impact of Your Parents' Divorce.* Hope4ACD Publishing, 2019.

Deal, Ron. *Preparing to Blend: The Couple's Guide to Becoming a Smart Stepfamily.* Bethany House Publishers, 2021.

Deal, Ron. *The Smart Stepfamily.* Bethany House Publishers, 2014.

Foster, Brooke Lea. *The Way They Were: Dealing With Your Parents' Divorce After a Lifetime of Marriage.* Three Rivers Press, 2006.

Gaspard, Terry and Tracy Clifford, *Daughters of Divorce: Overcome the Legacy of Your Parents' Breakup and Enjoy a Happy, Long-Lasting Relationship.* Sourcebooks, 2016.

Hart, Archibald. *Healing Adult Children of Divorce: Taking Care of Unfinished Business So You Can Be Whole Again.* Servant, 1991.

Hunt, June. *How to Rise Above Abuse.* Harvest House Publishers, 2010.

Hughes, Carol and Bruce Fredenburg. *Home Will Never Be the Same Again: A Guide for Adult Children of Gray Divorce.* Rowan & Littlefield, 2020.

Klein, Karen. *The Broken Circle: Children of Divorce and Separation.* CreateSpace Independent Publishing, 2013.

Marquardt, Elizabeth. *Between Two Worlds.* Crown, 2005.

Meola, Dr. Daniel and Bethany Meola. *Life-Giving Wounds: A Catholic Guild to Healing for Adult Children of Divorce or Separation.* Ignatius Press, 2023.

Miller, Leila. *Primal Loss: The Now-Adult Children of Divorce Speak.* LCB Publishing, 2017.

Neuman, M. Gary. *The Long Way Home: The Powerful 4-Step Plan for Adult Children of Divorce.* John Wiley & Sons, 2013.

Staal, Stephanie. *The Love They Lost: Living with the Legacy of Our Parents' Divorce.* Delacorte Press, 2000.

Trent, John. *Breaking the Cycle of Divorce: How Your Marriage Can Succeed Even If Your Parents' Didn't.* Tyndale, 2006.

Wallerstein, Judith. *The Unexpected Legacy of Divorce.* Hyperion, 2000.

Wright, H. Norman, *Healing for the Father Wound.* Bethany House Publishers, 2005.

NOTES

PREFACE

1. Leila Miller, *Primal Loss* (LCB Publishing, 2017), 10.

2. Jen Weaver, "24 Questions to Help You Plan for Your Future Marriage," August 13, 2024, Focus on the Family, www .focusonthefamily.com/marriage/24-questions-to-help-you -plan-for-your-future-marriage.

3. Lauren Reitsema, *In Their Shoes: Helping Parents Better Understand and Connect with Children of Divorce* (Bethany House Publishers, 2019), 28.

4. E. Mavis Hetherington and John Kelly, *For Better or for Worse: Divorce Reconsidered* (W. W. Norton & Co., 2002), 12.

CHAPTER 1

1. Kevin Leman, *What a Difference a Daddy Makes* (Thomas Nelson, 2001), 119.

2. Nicolas H. Wolfinger, *Understanding the Divorce Cycle* (Cambridge University Press, 2005), 106, 109

3. Ekateřina Volevach, "Transmission of Union Instability in 16 Countries: Comparison by Gender and Union Type," thesis, May 5, 2019, Masaryk University, https://is.muni.cz/th/y8ts5/.

4. Paul R. Amato, "Research on Divorce: Continuing Trends and New Developments," *Journal of Marriage and Family* 72, (2010): 650–66.

5. Susan E. Jacquet and Catherine A. Surra, "Parental Divorce and Premarital Couples: Commitment and Other Relationship Characteristics," *Journal of Marriage and Family* 63, no. 3 (2001): 627–38, https://doi.org/10.1111/j.1741-3737.2001.00627.x, in Terry Gaspard and Tracy Clifford, *Daughters of Divorce: Overcome the Legacy of Your Parents' Breakup and Enjoy a Happy, Long-Lasting Relationship* (Sourcebooks, 2016), xxix.

6. Sarah W. Whitton et al., "Effects of Parental Divorce on Marital Commitment and Confidence," *Journal of Family Psychology* 22, no. 5 (October 2008): 789-93, in Terry Gaspard and Tracy Clifford, *Daughters of Divorce: Overcome the Legacy of Your Parents' Breakup and Enjoy a Happy, Long-Lasting Relationship* (Sourcebooks, 2016), xxix.

7. E. Mavis Hetherington and John Kelly, *For Better or for Worse: Divorce Reconsidered* (W. W. Norton & Co., 2002), in Gaspard and Clifford, *Daughters of Divorce*, xxviii.

8. Leora E. Lawton and Regina Bures, "Parental Divorce and the 'Switching' of Religious Identity," *Journal for the Scientific Study of Religion* 40, no. 1 (March 2001): 106, quoted in Elizabeth Marquardt et al., *Does the Shape of Families Shape Faith?* (Institute for Family Values, 2013), 16, https://instituteforamericanvalues.org/catalog/pdfs/SOFSF.pdf.

9. Elizabeth Marquardt, "Between Two Worlds: The Inner Lives of Children of Divorce," 2010–2011 Word & World Lecture, *Word & World* 31, no. 2 (Luther Seminary, Spring 2011): 189.

10. Glenn Stanton, "Does Faith Reduce Divorce Risk?" *Public Discourse*, March 22, 2018, http://www.thepublicdiscourse.com /2018/03/20935/.

11. Annette Mahoney, et al., "Religion in the Home in the 1980s and 1990s: A Meta-Analytic Review and Conceptual Analysis of Links Between Religion, Marriage and Parenting," *Journal of Family Psychology* 15 (2001): 559–96, paraphrased and quoted in Stanton, "Does Faith Reduce Divorce Risk?", http:// www.thepublicdiscourse.com/2018/03/20935/.

CHAPTER 2

1. Brook Lea Foster, *The Way They Were: Dealing with Your Parents' Divorce After a Lifetime of Marriage* (Three Rivers Press, 2006), 3.

2. Susan L Brown, I-Fen Lin, "The Graying of Divorce: A Half Century of Change," *The Journals of Gerontology* Series B 77, no. 9 (2022): 1710–20, https://pubmed.ncbi.nlm.nih.gov/3538 5579/.

3. Natalia Camarena, "Parents' Divorce Affects Adult Children Too," *Sheridan Sun*, March 18, 2016, www.thesheridansun.ca /blog/2016/03/18/parents-divorce-affects-adult-children-too/.

4. Foster, *The Way They Were*, 26.

5. Carol R. Hughes and Bruce R. Fredenburg, *Home Will Never Be the Same Again: A Guide for Adult Children of Gray Divorce* (Rowman & Littlefield, 2020), 73.

6. Henry Cloud and John Townsend, *Boundaries*, rev. and upd. ed. (Zondervan, 2017).

CHAPTER 3

1. Tim LaHaye, *Anger Is a Choice* (Zondervan, 2002), 156.
2. Solangel Maldonado, "Taking Account of Children's Emotions: Anger and Forgiveness in 'Renegotiated Families,'" *Virginia Journal of Social Policy and the Law* 16, no. 443 (2009): 445, 447.
3. Maldonado, "Taking Account of Children's Emotions," 448.
4. Maldonado, "Taking Account of Children's Emotions," 448.
5. Maldonado, "Taking Account of Children's Emotions," 446.
6. Constance Ahrons, *The Good Divorce* (HarperCollins, 1994), 56, 57.
7. Maldonado, "Taking Account of Children's Emotions," 447.
8. Gary Chapman, *Anger: Handling a Powerful Emotion in a Healthy Way* (Northfield Publishing, 2007).

CHAPTER 4

1. Steven W. Banks, *Healing the Father-Wound* (Expanding Your Vision Publishers, 2009), 49.
2. Margo Maine, *Father Hunger: Fathers, Daughters, and the Pursuit of Thinness* (Gurze Books, 2004), 21.
3. Edward Teyber, *Helping Children Cope with Divorce* (Lexington Books, 1992), 108.
4. Information in this section adapted from Kent Darcie, "Father Hunger and the Search for Manhood," (blog), Hope4ADP,

n.d., https://hope4adp.com/father-hunger-and-the-search-for
-manhood/.

CHAPTER 5

1. Regina R, Robertson, ed., *He Never Came Home: Interviews, Stories, and Essays from Daughters on Life Without Their Fathers* (Agate Bolden, 2017), 100.
2. Neil Kalter, quoted in Tom Rodgers and Beverly Rodgers, *Adult Children of Divorced Parents: Making Your Marriage Work* (Resource Publications, 2002), 11.
3. Susan E. Jacquet and Catherine A. Surra, "Parental Divorce and Premarital Couples: Commitment and Other Relationship Characteristics," *Journal of Marriage and Family* 63, no. 3 (2001): 627–38, https://doi.org/10.1111/j.1741-3737.2001.00627.x, in Terry Gaspard and Tracy Clifford, *Daughters of Divorce: Overcome the Legacy of Your Parents' Breakup and Enjoy a Happy, Long-Lasting Relationship* (Sourcebooks, 2016), xxix.
4. Gaspard and Clifford, *Daughters of Divorce*, 8.
5. Kevin Leman, *What a Difference a Daddy Makes* (Thomas Nelson, 2001), 119.
6. *Enhanced Strong's Lexicon*, s.v. "precious," Libronix Digital Library System.

CHAPTER 6

1. W. D. Manning and L. Carlson (2021), "Trends in Cohabitation Prior to Marriage," Family Profiles, FP-21-04, National

Center for Family & Marriage Research, https://doi.org/10
.25035/ncfmr/fp-21-04.

2. Theresa E. DiDonato, "3 Questions Every Couple Must
Answer Before Moving in Together," March 27, 2022,
https://www.psychologytoday.com/us/blog/meet-catch-and
-keep/202203/3-questions-every-couple-must-answer-moving
-in-together.

3. William G. Axinn and Jennifer S. Barber, "Living Arrange-
ments and Family Formation Attitudes in Early Adulthood,"
Journal of Marriage and the Family 59, no. 3 (1997): 595–
611, in Wendy D. Manning and Jessica A. Cohen, *Cohabitation and Marital Dissolution: The Significance of Marriage
Cohort*, Department of Sociology & Center for Family
and Demographic Research, Bowling Green State University, n.d., https://paa2011.populationassociation.org/papers
/112067, 6.

4. Glenn T. Stanton, *The Ring Makes All the Difference* (Moody
Publishers, 2011), 66, 67.

5. Chris M. Wilson and Andrew J. Oswald, "How Does Marriage
Affect Physical and Psychological Health? A Survey of the Lon-
gitudinal Evidence," University of Warwick (May 5, 2005), in
Stanton, *Hidden Consequences of Cohabitation*, 66.

6. Michael S. Pollard and Kathleen Mullan Harris, "Cohabitation and Marriage Intensity: Consolidation, Intimacy, and
Commitment," June 28, 2013, RAND working paper series
WR-1001, in Terry Gaspard, "Living Together Versus Marriage: Benefits and Risks Over the Long Run," *Huffpost,*

updated May 7, 2017, https://www.huffpost.com/entry/living
-together-versus-ma_b_9854344.

7. Amanda Chatel, "9 Ways Your Life Changes Once You Move
in Together," *Bustle*, July 6, 2016, https://www.bustle.com
/articles/170786-9-ways-your-life-changes-once-you-move-in
-together.

8. Mario Canseco, "Canadian Couples Did Mostly Well Cohabiting During Pandemic," *Research Co.*, September 20, 2022,
https://researchco.ca/2022/09/20/covid19-couples-canada/.

9. Mike McManus and Harriet McManus, *Living Together:
Myths, Risks & Answers* (Howard Books, 2008), 21.

10. Daniel T. Lichter and Zhenchao Qian, "Serial Cohabitation
and the Marital Life Course," *Journal of Marriage and Family*
70, no. 4 (November 2008): 861–78, quoted in Stanton, *Hidden Consequences of Cohabitation*, 67.

11. Rick Kirby, "What Is the True Meaning of Fornication in the
Bible?" Bible Study Tools, updated March 24, 2022, https://
www.biblestudytools.com/bible-study/topical-studies/what-is
-the-sin-fornication.html.

CHAPTER 7

1. Jen Abbas, *Generation EX: Adult Children of Divorce and the
Healing of Our Pain* (Waterbrook Press, 2004), 22.

2. Gary Neuman, *The Long Way Home: The Powerful 4-Step Plan
for Adult Children of Divorce* (Trade Paper Press, 2013), 74.

3. Neuman, *The Long Way Home*, 75.

4. Daniel Meola and Bethany Meola, *Life-Giving Wounds: A Catholic Guide to Healing for Adult Children of Divorce or Separation* (Ignatius Press, 2023), 134.

5. Nicolas H. Wolfinger, "Counterintuitive Trends in the Link Between Premarital Sex and Marital Stability," Institute for Family Studies, June 6, 2016, https://ifstudies.org/blog/counterintuitive-trends-in-the-link-between-prema+rital-sex-and-marital-stability.

6. Jason S. Carrol and Brian J. Willoughby, "The Myth of Sexual Experience," Institute for Family Studies, April 18, 2023, https://ifstudies.org/blog/the-myth-of-sexual-experience-.

7. David C. Reardon, "The Abortion and Mental Health Controversy: A Comprehensive Literature Review of Common Ground Agreements, Disagreements, Actional Recommendations, and Research Opportunities," SAGE Open Medicine 6 (2018): 1–38, https://journals.sagepub.com/doi/pdf/10.1177/2050312118807624.

8. Brenda Major et al., *Report of the APA Task Force on Mental Health and Abortion*, American Psychological Association (2008), https://www.apa.org/pi/women/programs/abortion/mental-health.pdf.

CHAPTER 8

1. Daniel Meola and Bethany Meola, *Life-Giving Wounds: A Catholic Guide to Healing for Adult Children of Divorce or Separation* (Ignatius Press, 2023), 123.

2. Dave Wilson and Ann Wilson, hosts, *FamilyLife Today* podcast, "Approaching Marriage," October 9, 2013, https://

www.familylife.com/podcast/familylife-today/approaching-marriage/.

3. Ron Deal, Smart Stepfamily Therapy Provider training, May 2021.

4. Constance Ahrons, *The Good Divorce* (HarperCollins, 1994), 52–57.

5. Jen Abbas, *Generation EX: Adult Children of Divorce and the Healing of Our Pain* (Waterbrook Press, 2004), 18.

6. Stephanie Staal, *The Love They Lost: Living with the Legacy of Our Parents' Divorce* (Delacorte Press, 2000), 203.

7. Daniel Meola and Bethany Meola, *Life-Giving Wounds: A Catholic Guide to Healing for Adult Children of Divorce or Separation* (Ignatius Press, 2023), 91.

8. Jack Balswick and Judith Balswick, *The Family: A Christian Perspective on the Contemporary Home* (Baker Academic, 1999), 26.

9. Jim Daly, *Why Family Matters: A Modern Look at an Ancient Truth* (Focus on the Family, 2013), 40–41.

CHAPTER 9

1. Beverly Rodgers and Tom Rodgers, *Adult Children of Divorced Parents: Making Your Marriage Work* (Resource Publications, 2002), 76.

2. Jack Balswick and Judith Balswick, *The Family: A Christian Perspective on the Contemporary Home* (Baker Academic, 1999), 79.

CHAPTER 11

1. E. Mavis Hetherington and John Kelly, *For Better or for Worse: Divorce Reconsidered* (W. W. Norton & Co., 2002), 193.

2. A. W. Geiger and Gretchen Livingston, "8 Facts About Love and Marriage in America," Pew Research Center, February 13, 2019, https://www.pewresearch.org/short-reads/2019/02/13/8-facts-about-love-and-marriage/, in Christy Bieber, "Revealing Divorce Statistics in 2023," *Forbes*, n.d., https://www.forbes.com/advisor/legal/divorce/divorce-statistics/#sources_section.

3. Lauren Reitsema, *In Their Shoes: Helping Parents Better Understand and Connect with Children of Divorce* (Bethany House Publishers, 2019), 15–16.

CHAPTER 12

1. Jann Blackstone-Ford and Sharyl Jupe, *Ex-etiquette for Weddings: The Blended Families' Guide to Tying the Knot* (Chicago Review Press, 2007), 134.

CHAPTER 13

1. Focus on the Family, *The Masterpiece Marriage* (Bethany House, 2014), 23.

ABOUT THE AUTHOR

KENT DARCIE, LPC is the founder and president of Adult Children of Divorce Ministries. He is a Licensed Professional Counselor, author, popular speaker, and has been interviewed on podcasts and other programs. He has presented teachings and workshops on the issues that impact adults with divorced parents since 2004. He also wrote and recorded a series of programs on the issues faced by adults with divorced parents for Trans World Radio (TWR) which have been heard around the world in multiple languages. Kent is committed to helping adults with divorced parents minimize the impact of their parents' divorce by offering resources and tools that facilitate restored and healthy relationships with God, themselves, their spouse, and others.

He and his wife, Kathy, have been married for more than forty years and have three grown children. Kent can be contacted through the website: Hope4ADP.com.